Praise for *Hope Is a Bright Star*

"Alternately wrenching and hopeful . . . The book itself is crafted . . . as an act of love and of healing . . . Wilcox and her daughters' story is unique and memorable, evoking deep emotion within the reader. *Hope Is a Bright Star* stands as an often moving account of loss and perseverance. . . . the detailed passages concerning Elizabeth's diagnosis, treatment, and memory prove raw and moving."

—The Booklife Prize

"*Hope Is a Bright Star* is an account of the healing and profound growth that can follow deep loss. Wilcox captures her experience with tight, evocative language and imagery that doesn't hold back the painful parts but reminds us of how courageous and resilient we can be as she brings us along on her journey toward hope and life. Throughout, we are reminded of the healing power of nature, the merciful insistence of hope, and the lasting power of love."

—Blyth Lord, founder and executive director of
the Courageous Parents Network

Hope Is a Bright Star

Hope Is a Bright Star

Bright Star

A Mother's Memoir
of Love, Loss, and
Learning to Live Again

Faith Fuller Wilcox

Faith Fuller Wilcox

SHE WRITES PRESS

Published 2021
Printed in the United States of America
Print ISBN: 978-1-64742-108-3
E-ISBN: 978-1-64742-109-0
Library of Congress Control Number: 2020922180

For information, address:
She Writes Press
1569 Solano Ave #546
Berkeley, CA 94707

She Writes Press is a division of SparkPoint Studio, LLC.

Names of the medical professionals and several individuals are changed to protect confidentiality.

To Olivia and Elizabeth—
I will love you always.

And to my family and community—
Your love and support rescued me.

Contents

Part 1: "I Never Knew"

Part 2: "Night Sky"

Part 3: "Destiny"

Foreword

"**M**ay I start by reading a chapter?" Faith asks quietly.
"Of course," I say gently, knowing that Faith's writing
expresses the core of her grief for her fourteen-year-old daughter
who died, and for the painful and challenging journey she's been on
to build a life after being shattered by the loss.

Faith's tears come in the midst of the reading. She reaches for the
tissues and presses on; each word, each line, is a mother's keening cry.
As I open to the heartbroken woman in front of me, tears well up in
my eyes. Faith looks up at me, her eyes revealing a bottomless well of
grief. For a moment, there is a pure silence between us, beyond words.

I have been privileged to be Faith's therapist throughout her
daughter's illness and untimely death and during the many years of
Faith's grieving and healing. There is no greater loss for anyone than
the loss of a child. It is what all parents fear the most. I have seen
Faith confront and ultimately learn how to face this fear and bear the
unbearable.

Faith's book, *Hope Is a Bright Star*, represents the completion of
her healing journey. Not that her heart doesn't ache every day with
the loss of Elizabeth. She knows she will always feel that pain. But she
also knows that one must go on. Faith utilizes the telling of her story

to make words, meaning, and even beauty out of the nightmare that engulfed her child and her family. Each chapter is a teardrop and a prism. Each chapter is a step toward the light. Each chapter is an act of faith.

Faith has written down her tears to grieve her loss and to share it with you that you might feel connection and compassion for your own losses too. She knows that grieving alone lasts forever, and grieving together heals. Thank you, Faith, for your gift to us all.

—David Treadway, PhD

Preface

O ne year—365 days to be exact—was like no other in my life or the lives of my daughters. My youngest daughter, Elizabeth, was diagnosed with osteosarcoma, a rare bone cancer that afflicts only one in every 250,000 children each year. Sometimes, I try to imagine what it would look like to have a quarter of a million children stand at the edge of a crevasse, and only one child, my spirited thirteen-year-old daughter, be forced to take the terrifying step over the edge.

Not only did Elizabeth's diagnosis shock me, but it also forced me to face my domineering then-husband. I gained a sudden strength to move with my daughters to my sister's home. In time, I was divorced and was able to fulfill a dream and buy a home for my daughters and me.

We were safe at my sister's and had the support of family and friends. We had the expertise of an army of highly specialized doctors and nurses. And Olivia, eighteen months older than her sister and inseparable from her, was constantly by her bedside. We all tried to save Elizabeth with every resource we could find and every medical procedure the health professionals could administer. Elizabeth held on for one harrowing year, but the pain of her multiplying tumors and the exhaustion brought on by eleven months of nonstop treatments was too much.

For Olivia and me to go on, I had to harness what little strength was left within. I drew upon one whisper of me that remained—an almost extinguished voice that emerged when I began to write. As I confronted the harsh landscape of the traumas of our past, I was not alone. With the unwavering love of my family and friends and the guidance of my wise counselor, over time I slowly crossed the scarred terrain.

This is the story of a family fractured by the life-threatening illness and death of one of its daughters . . . a family held together by a community of relatives and friends . . . a diminished family who survived grief and reclaimed their lives.

Note: Poems are the original work of the author.

Part 1
"I Never Knew"

I never knew heart-stopping shock before.
I never knew the nauseating, plunging collapse
following grave diagnoses.
I never knew that sleep could flee even after exhaustion
sets in.
I never knew how to administer medical procedures.
I never knew the overwhelming responsibility
of trying to keep my children alive, safe, and together.

But even in this darkest of times,
I do know that the love of my family and friends
is carrying me over perilous terrain.
I do know that the doctors, nurses, and social workers are
working
beyond all measure to save Elizabeth.

I do know that a reservoir of strength resides within me.
And I vow that I will never cease
comforting, learning, striving
to save my children,
to save our trinity.

Chapter 1

Shock

July 2000

She springs off the starting blocks, dives into the water, and swims rapidly down the racing lane. She's the anchor of the freestyle relay team, and with her long reach, strong strokes, and powerful kick, she moves into the lead. At the end of the lane, she flips and pushes forward, eager to earn first place for her team. On the return lap, her pace slows. The competitor in the next lane takes the lead. Seconds later, she slaps the wall, finishing in second place. She lifts herself up to sit on the edge of the pool.

I wrap a towel around her. "That was a great race, Elizabeth."

"Thanks, Mom, but I was running out of breath. Can we go home now? I'm exhausted."

On the ride home, I remember Elizabeth's recent annual checkup when she asked her doctor, "My right knee was sore when I played soccer last spring, and it's not any better now. Do you know why?"

He pressed around her knee and said, "It could be growing pains. A year ago, you were five six, and today you're five nine. Many kids your age who have growth spurts have similar pains. We can do a follow-up if the pain continues. Is everything else okay?"

"Well, not really. My lungs hurt when I ride my bike and sometimes when I swim."

1

Her doctor placed the stethoscope on her back and asked her to take deep breaths. "I'm checking for any fluid in your lungs because that can be painful, but your lungs are clear. I don't know why they hurt."

Even though we left with a few unanswered questions, we both felt relieved when the checkup didn't indicate anything unusual.

Now four weeks later, I'm worried. Elizabeth's right knee looks swollen, and after seeing her tire out quickly during her swimming race, I decide to get a second opinion.

I bring Elizabeth to a doctor who specializes in orthopedics. He takes an X-ray of her right knee and says that he'll let us know the results. A few days later I get a call, but to my surprise, instead of hearing the voice of the orthopedic doctor, it's our pediatrician.

"The X-ray revealed a shadow around Elizabeth's right knee," he says with urgency. "She needs to have an MRI and be seen by an orthopedic doctor tomorrow. I'll make the appointments, and this afternoon you'll get a call from my office with details."

I don't have a chance to ask any questions.

I'm confused. Why did our pediatrician call me, not the orthopedic doctor, and what does "a shadow around her knee" mean? My stomach churns. Something's wrong.

Elizabeth walks into the kitchen and asks, "Mommy, was that the doctor? What did he say?"

I quickly gather my composure and respond, "The X-ray showed something unusual, and you're going to have an MRI tomorrow. Later, we'll meet with a different orthopedic doctor at the hospital, and after he sees the images, he can tell us more."

She asks, "What else did he tell you?"

"Nothing more except we'll know when and where to go for your MRI before the end of the afternoon."

When Elizabeth goes upstairs to tell Olivia, I go downstairs to my husband Neville's studio. He's concentrating on repairing a camera lens. When I tell him the news, he brushes it off and says, "It's probably nothing."

"Will you go to the hospital with us tomorrow?"

"If you want me to."

The next day, Elizabeth winces as the medical technicians position her leg for the MRI. Before the procedure begins, she gives me a radiant smile to reassure me.

Neville and I are in the waiting room. I'm anxious; he looks oddly unconcerned. An hour later, Elizabeth walks out of the exam room on crutches, her right knee hurting after being in the same position for so long. As instructed, we go to the next appointment. The placard next to the door reads, DR. HERBERT, ORTHOPEDIC ONCOLOGY. In shock, I look at my husband and quickly shuffle Elizabeth into the office so she can't see this sign. She picks up a fashion magazine, and I listen to the conversations around me. One woman, whose leg has been amputated at the knee, leans toward the person next to her and says, "I've talked to you before. Are you feeling better?"

"Yes, my headaches are almost gone after my neck surgery."

My heart is racing; my husband's expression is blank. Does he realize the implications of our being in an oncology office?

Dr. Herbert is in his midseventies and has a gentlemanly manner. He asks a resident to examine Elizabeth, and when he presses hard on her knee, she screams. Dr. Herbert is furious and asks the resident to leave. The doctor apologizes and very gently examines her knee. Finally, he tells us that there is a growth in the area. He wants her to have some blood drawn and a CT scan this evening. She slumps forward, shaking. Dr. Herbert suggests she use a wheelchair to get to the lab and to the room for the CT scan.

As I push her in the wheelchair, I say, "Elizabeth, I know these appointments are scary and all you want to do is to go home now. But we need to find out more about your knee. You're being so brave.

We'll be with you the whole time." I bend down and kiss the top of her head, inwardly reeling with the enormity of what is unfolding.

When the nurse wheels Elizabeth to have her blood drawn, I call my mother and my father, a retired internist. "We are at the hospital, and the doctors just told us that Elizabeth has a growth near her knee. It could be cancer. She has to have a CT scan, but it can't be done until seven o'clock. She's exhausted and hurting. I need to go now, but I'll call you again when I know more. I just can't believe this!"

I also call the friend with whom Olivia is spending the day to ask if she can take her home because we won't get there until nine o'clock. She agrees.

Neville has gone into another room to call a friend. He looks troubled and gives me the silent treatment. I know he's not pleased that I called my parents because he's had a long-standing aversion to them. I've been unsuccessful over the years in repairing the antagonistic relationship between them.

It's dark outside now, and I feel suspended in time. Silently I wonder, *Oh, my baby, my baby, what is going on?* Elizabeth sits by my side and leans into me as we wait for the next appointment.

The CT scan is finished by eight, and then we all drive home. Neville is silent. Elizabeth is exhausted and in pain. I talk quietly and gently with her. Olivia runs to the car when we get home. She and I help Elizabeth out of the back seat, and she uses the hospital crutches to slowly walk down the path and up the few stairs into our house. Once she is settled in bed, Olivia sits by her sister's side. I can hear them talking quietly as I lie sleeplessly in mine.

The following morning, Dr. Herbert calls. "I'm so sorry to tell you that Elizabeth does have cancer, but we don't yet know if it's Ewing's sarcoma or osteosarcoma."

"What is the difference?" I ask.

"With Ewing's sarcoma, cancerous tumors grow in bones or in the soft tissue around bones. And while serious, it has a more successful outcome with treatment. With osteosarcoma, cancerous tumors grow in the wide ends of long bones like the femur or humerus. That disease is tenacious and harder to treat."

I ask what will happen next, and Dr. Herbert explains the upcoming procedure. After I put the phone down, Olivia and Elizabeth immediately ask, "What did the doctor say? Tell us the truth, Mommy." Ever since they were very young, I've taught them the importance of telling the truth, and I do so now.

I look at Elizabeth and say, "You have a type of sarcoma cancer, but they don't know which kind yet."

"Will I have chemotherapy? Will I have surgery? What's next, Mommy?"

"Dr. Herbert has set up one more test so they can determine which type of cancer you have. They've scheduled a procedure for Friday morning, when they'll remove a piece of bone from your femur. Then several days later, they'll tell us which sarcoma you have."

I tightly hug my stunned daughters.

In a daze, I walk downstairs to tell Neville, who is in his photography studio. Olivia follows me. I tell him the horrifying news. His face turns dull gray, and he remains speechless as we talk to him. He makes no attempt to get up and comfort Olivia or me. Then it hits me—I'll have to be the one to carry my family through this crisis.

Chapter 2
Ten Percent
August 25, 2000

O ur phones are in constant use over the next few days. Elizabeth calls her friends; Olivia calls hers. The parents of their friends call me. I call my sisters, my parents, and Neville's mother. We are all stunned with this new reality. Friends visit our home and bring gifts; parents bring over meals. Despite all of the hugs and expressions of support, it's too much activity for Elizabeth. She's exhausted.

When I tell my friend Lisa about Elizabeth's diagnosis, she says without hesitation, "I'll be there with you, Olivia, and Elizabeth when the procedure happens."

The day before the test Neville asks me, "Do I need to go?"

I hesitate and then say, "No," thinking to myself that if he doesn't want to be there with his daughters and me, if he doesn't understand his family's need for his support, then I don't want him there.

When my sister Susie hears that I'm driving us to the hospital, she says, "I'll drive you to the hospital, stay with all three of you until the end of the day, and bring you back home." I don't find out until later that, because I'm in a state of shock, Susie doesn't think it's safe for me to drive.

As we enter the hospital, Olivia pushes her sister's wheelchair into the busy lobby. Lisa, Susie, and Susie's thirteen-year-old daughter, Robin, are by my side.

First, we meet with Dr. Herbert. He leans toward Elizabeth and asks how she feels; then he clearly explains the upcoming procedure in simple terms.

A nurse helps Elizabeth slide onto a stretcher. Olivia and I walk beside her to the room where she will receive conscious sedation, a type of anesthesia. Dr. Herbert and a young resident wheel Elizabeth into an operating room. She smiles at Olivia and me as if to say, "I know it's going to be okay."

Lisa leaves to do an errand, and Olivia, Susie, Robin, and I take a pedestrian bridge over Storrow Drive to sit under a tree along the edge of the Charles River. It's a hot day, and Robin and Olivia have brought their Rollerblades to skate on the path along the Esplanade. As I watch people riding their bikes, jogging, and walking by, it strikes me that I'm living in two realities. Along the river, people are enjoying a summer day while, just over the bridge, my youngest is undergoing a procedure to identify her life-threatening illness. After a few minutes of silence, I turn to Susie and ask, "If we have to come back to the hospital next week, can you bring us, please?"

Susie replies, "I'll be there for you every day for the rest of my life."

After an hour and a half, we all walk back to the hospital, where Lisa joins us. We go to the recovery room to see Elizabeth. She tells us that the procedure was "not bad—*really*." The resident avoids my eyes. And then I know. I know before they tell us the type of cancer Elizabeth has; it's osteosarcoma.

I am hurtling into a world from which I want to flee. I want to grab Elizabeth and run away with her, run to a place where children are healthy, run to a place with no pain or suffering. Elizabeth's voice pulls me back. "Mommy, you know they can give me an artificial knee like they gave Nana. I'll be okay."

Unable to speak, I squeeze her hand.

Dr. Herbert and Dr. Kin, a pediatric oncologist whom we're meeting for the first time, ask us all to go into a room where we can talk.

They tell us that they do not need to wait for the results of the biopsy; Elizabeth does have osteosarcoma. Stunned, none of us speaks for quite a while. Then I ask, "Can you tell us what this means?"

Dr. Kin replies, "Elizabeth will need at least ten months of treatments, beginning with intensive chemotherapy, possibly surgery and radiation. In fact, as this disease is so tenacious, the treatments might last for as long as one year."

Elizabeth asks, "What kind of surgery?"

Dr. Herbert answers, "We would replace your femur."

It's hard for me to hear the rest of what is said. I lean against the wall for support, and my heart pounds so hard that I begin to shake. Everyone looks shocked, our eyes filling with tears. I wish they had not told us so bluntly, in front of three young children.

Elizabeth sits up and looks deeply into my eyes. I hold her hand. Then she turns to the doctors and asks, "What is my chance of survival?"

"About ten percent."

Chapter 3

Looking Back

Mid-1980s

A s the news about Elizabeth's illness spreads, my closest friends and sisters call each other frequently and brainstorm about how they can provide support to Elizabeth, Olivia, and me. From the very beginning, I know that this band of caring and strong women will help me and my daughters through every trial that lies ahead.

Lisa has always been there for me. She was my closest friend in high school, and after we graduated from college, we both lived in Boston, where our friendship grew even stronger. During this time, I was married, and two years later I was pregnant with my first child. One night, when Lisa was having dinner at our Beacon Hill apartment, I mentioned that I wanted to go to childbirth classes. My husband looked away and showed no interest in participating. A moment later Lisa said, "I'll go with you. I'd like to!"

So, once a week, we climbed into her VW Jetta, drove to Brookline, and attended classes at a local hospital. At one of our last classes, the teacher asked me, "Who will be your birthing coach?" I didn't know what to say.

Lisa piped up, "I will be."

Within one week, I called Lisa and said, "It's time." I vividly remember gripping Lisa's hand during the fiercest contractions, and

Lisa coaching me about when to breathe. Neville lay on a stretcher behind a curtain, saying that he had a bad case of indigestion. Thirteen hours of labor later, I gave birth to Olivia.

I had been nervous about Neville's reaction, but he beamed when he held his firstborn child. I asked Lisa to be her godmother.

During the years that followed, Lisa and I shared many days together with Olivia and Elizabeth, who was born eighteen months after her sister. Lisa came to my children's birthday parties, drove us into the country to her uncle's farm to show my girls domestic animals, and included us in Sunday dinners at her grandmother's house.

I had solo times with Lisa too. She was the only one I shared my feelings with about being married to an angry man who always put me down. As the years passed, my girls felt his domineering ways too, and little by little they withdrew from him, which only made him more demanding and unreasonable.

Chapter 4

Reeling

September 2000

"**Y**ou have to wear this suit if you want to go with your daughter into the operating room."

I step into the one-piece coverall that envelops my legs, torso, and arms and zip it up to my chin. I slip on blue cotton slippers and a mask that covers my nose and mouth. My father is by my side, clad in a similar protective suit. Elizabeth is on a stretcher, and I hold her hand as she is pushed into the pre-op area. This is a major surgery to implant a central line needed for her chemotherapy treatments.

I watch as a nurse inserts a thin tube into a vein on Elizabeth's arm and connects it to an IV for painkillers and a relaxant. Drop by drop Elizabeth becomes groggy and slips into sleep. The surgeon explains the upcoming procedure to my father and me. He will insert a central line into a central vein. At the opposite end, the central line will have two exterior branches: one branch for drawing blood, and the other for giving chemotherapy. I grab my father's hand as we listen. When we leave the pre-op room, I'm sobbing; a few weeks ago, Elizabeth was happily swimming in a pool with friends.

When Elizabeth wakes up, we are in a room on one of the pediatric floors. I can see the Esplanade along the Charles River, where Susie and I sat last week. The view from the room is as lovely as a view from one of Boston's luxury hotels, but this is about as far away from relaxation as one could possibly be.

Elizabeth stirs and, in her still-foggy mind, tries to stand up and walk by herself. After a few steps she falters, and I rush over to hold up her limp body. The nurse appears, and we carry Elizabeth back to bed.

The next night, August 31, Elizabeth is given her first round of chemotherapy. The doctors told us that they will give her intensive chemotherapy right from the start because she has stage IV cancer. It's brutal. For six days, she sleeps day and night.

The first time the nurse changes Elizabeth's central-line dressing, I see a white plastic tube about eighteen inches long protruding out of the right side of her chest. Halfway down the tube, it divides into two, and the ends of these branches have caps—one red and one blue. Large black stitches stretch over her skin like a spider's grasping legs, keeping the tube in position. I feel myself falling but manage to land on a chair.

The nurse's voice comes to me as if from far away and instructs me about how to remove the Tegaderm, a clear plastic-like square covering the incision, and then clean the affected area, "flush" the double lumen lines by injecting solutions of saline and heparin, and cover the area of the surgery with a new, sterile Tegaderm dressing. *But I'm just the mother*, I want to say. *I'm not a trained nurse! I don't think I can do this.*

How am I ever going to learn all of these medical procedures that I'll need to take care of my child? In less than a week Elizabeth will be home, and I will have to change her dressing, flush her lines, watch out for warning signs (such as fevers), give a nutrient-rich fluid by IV, and give her the necessary shots to boost her immune system to fight infections. Am I capable enough to handle all of these medical tasks *and* provide comfort to Elizabeth and Olivia as we struggle through these treatments and long hospital stays?

Why, God, why is this all happening? How can it be that only two months ago, Elizabeth was enjoying the first carefree days of school vacation, and now she is lying in a hospital bed gravely ill? God, why can't You transport her back to the time when she was well *before these cancerous cells invaded her body?*

At the end of the weekend, Elizabeth, still in bed, asks for a bowl of warm water, and she washes her pale face. Then she brushes her teeth. This is the most activity she has done in a week. Buoyed by her efforts, she asks for a clean T-shirt. As an adolescent who never wears an item of clothing for more than one day, she is horrified that she has been wearing the same T-shirt for almost a week. After this makeshift toilette, she feels refreshed, and her spirits rise a bit.

On the seventh day, we bring Elizabeth home. She's thin and frail, but her engaging smile dispels some of my worries. Olivia helps her out of the wheelchair and onto the sofa in the family room. I cook shrimp, Elizabeth's favorite food. After eating two shrimps, she says, "Thank you, but that's enough for now."

Concerned about her flushed face, I take her temperature. The thermometer reads over one hundred degrees. Following his earlier instruction, I call Dr. Kin, and he says to bring Elizabeth back to the hospital. My heart sinks, and Elizabeth starts to cry. Neither of us has the strength for another ordeal.

About eight that night, Olivia and I support Elizabeth as we slowly walk to the car. At the hospital, they have a double room ready for us on the other pediatric floor. A newborn infant is in the section next to hers. I draw the curtain around Elizabeth and me to form a U-shaped cocoon.

Dr. Kin enters, and Elizabeth gives him a weak smile. "I'm sorry you had to come back here, Elizabeth, but we need to give you fluids to bring your fever down. We'll set up the IV and won't have to disturb you very often. You should have a quiet night." Elizabeth nods and soon goes to sleep.

From the gap in the curtain, I see a Japanese gentleman in his late sixties stop at the door. He takes off his shoes, slides on slippers, and steps into the room. A stunning woman, perhaps his daughter, follows him. The man approaches the opening in the curtain and bows. I smile and step toward him. In a muted voice he says, "My grandson was born yesterday with an abnormality in his stomach. Would you like to see him? He is a handsome boy, my first grandchild." I'm surprised but agree.

In the room, the mother quietly weeps as she holds her baby swaddled in a blanket. His eyes are closed, and tufts of downy black hair cover his head. He is so still—no babbling or crying—still like the sea in a dead calm without a breath of wind. "He's a lovely child," I say. The grandfather's eyes meet mine, and he bows his head in wordless thanks for showing compassion for his vulnerable grandchild.

A week later, Elizabeth returns home. The twenty-mile drive exhausts her. She opens the car door, puts her right arm around my shoulder, and hops forward on her left leg. Her right leg, where the massive tumor is growing near her knee, is too weak to support her. Slowly, we make it up the stairs, and she falls into her bed.

This is the first night that I need to nurse Elizabeth on my own. I give her nausea and pain medication and set up an IV to give her the infusion for nourishment. I bend over to kiss her forehead, and she wraps her arms around my neck. "I love you, Mommy."

"I love you too."

An ear-shattering buzzing wakes me in the night. The alarm connected to the pump for the IV is alerting me that the central line is blocked; I don't know why. I shut off the alarm, and Elizabeth is so groggy she falls back to sleep. I read and reread the instructions, my eyes blurring with tears. I can't understand. . . . I'm not trained to do this. I call the number on the instruction sheet, and a nurse answers. Step by step I follow the procedure that she counts out for me. I restart the pump, but the alarm starts ringing again. The nurse sounds annoyed and starts to repeat the instructions gruffly. I begin to cry. "I'm operating this pump for the first time. . . . My thirteen-year-old child is so sick she is suffering. . . . I'm trying, I'm trying."

The voice on the other end of the line is silent for a few moments, and then she says, "I'm sorry. Let's try again."

During the entire night, my husband growls angrily when the alarm goes off. The second time, he says harshly, "I'll fix it!"

When she sees her father, Elizabeth looks at me anxiously. After reading the instructions, he gives up, hands them to me, and goes back to bed. I'm able to find out what went wrong and then restart the process. When I slip into bed, he announces, "We can't be interrupted all night long like this again!"

The following morning, as Olivia gets ready for high school, I give her a big hug in the kitchen. She, too, is losing weight, and she looks tired. "Mom, will you be home tonight? You've been away so much, and I miss you."

"I've been missing you too, honey. I know that I haven't spent much time with you over the past two weeks, and I'm sorry."

"I understand, Mom, but it's hard to be home without you and only with Dad. He either spends hours and hours at night doing his work or talking to his friends on the phone. He's in a bad mood all the time."

"I know; it's terrible. I'll try to figure out something better. Perhaps your grandmother could have dinner with you more often, or you can have a friend for an overnight. I'll pick you up at school at the end of the day." The honking of a car ends our conversation. Olivia goes out and gets into a car with the high school junior I've hired to give her rides in the morning.

A new routine unfolds as we adjust to Elizabeth's condition. We start each day with our familiar embrace. She props herself up in bed, and I bring a bowl filled with warm water, a clean facecloth, her toothbrush and toothpaste, and a bowl so she can rinse out her mouth. Then I bring Elizabeth her makeup bag and a small mirror. She thinks about what she could eat, what will stay down. While I'm in the kitchen making her breakfast, she turns on her radio, changes her pj's, and puts on her makeup. I bring in her breakfast tray, pull up a chair, and keep her company.

Today it almost seems as though Elizabeth is just home with the flu. Our conversation revolves around her friends and what she might like to do on the weekend. And then the school bus drives by our house. Instead of stopping in front, as it has done for the past seven years, it keeps going. Elizabeth looks at me, her eyes brimming with tears.

Chapter 5

Breaking Up and Being Held

Early Fall 2000

Olivia is in her freshman year of high school, and while it is hard for her, she is trying her best to keep her life at school on a familiar path. She's a bright and focused student, always asking questions in class, often leading group projects, and usually achieving As. The freshman class of four hundred students is enormous compared to her eighth-grade class of fifty in middle school, but Olivia is ready to make new friends.

She visits Elizabeth in the hospital as often as she can, but it is challenging for her to get there at the end of the school day. And even if a friend of mine gives her a ride, the reality is that seeing Elizabeth lying in bed with multiple IVs or retching after days of chemotherapy tears Olivia apart. Elizabeth is more than her sister—she's her best friend, her constant companion throughout her life.

Often when Elizabeth is sedated, Olivia holds her hand, and in her pure soprano voice softly sings, "Over the Sea to Skye." Their paternal grandmother used to sing this ballad when they were toddlers as they were falling asleep at night. Hearing Olivia sing this song to her sister takes me back to innocent times.

And so, Olivia bounces back and forth between two worlds—one filled with active days in school with her classmates, the other with evenings at the hospital with her suffering sister or at home with her querulous father. Even in this time of crisis, he continues to be short-tempered and harsh.

Neville never tolerated points of view other than his own. Once, we replaced a tired carpet with hardwood floors in the downstairs of our condominium. When it was time to do the upstairs, the girls and I explicitly said that we wanted new carpets, not hardwood floors, which Neville wanted. One day I returned from work to discover that the carpets upstairs had been torn up and new hardwood floors were being installed. Stacks of wood flooring filled Olivia's bedroom and the master bedroom.

He had had his way. I wept.

Now with a torn heart, only one week after we've been home, I leave Olivia again and drive Elizabeth to the hospital for her second round of chemotherapy. I didn't know there were so many different types of chemotherapy, a plethora of combinations. The doctors are brutally truthful with me: there is no standard protocol for treating osteosarcoma. Together a team of pediatric oncologists make their best decisions based on their experiences with other patients with the same diagnosis.

The doctors' lack of certainty about how to treat this illness makes me feel like the solid ground Elizabeth and I once stood on has split into a wide divide, and we are sliding down. Do the doctors have the knowledge to save Elizabeth? Will she have the stamina and will to endure all of the treatments? Do I have the strength that it will take to comfort and support Olivia too?

This round of intensive chemotherapy turns out to be brutal for Elizabeth. The doctors have chosen methotrexate and cisplatin, two of the harshest drugs available, to arrest the rapidly growing primary tumor in her right leg. A few days after her infusions, she has a CT scan and chest X-ray. The doctors report the good news that Elizabeth's primary tumor has not grown in the last three weeks. The bad news they tell us is that she has numerous small tumors in her lungs. We'd been told osteosarcoma can metastasize to the lungs. We're crushed.

Elizabeth says to Dr. Kin, "So that's why I had pain in my chest when I did my swimming races."

"Yes."

That's all the oncologists reveal now. I wonder if there is more to tell us but they're waiting because we can't handle any harsher news.

During the end of this seven-day hospital stay, my elder sister, Sarah, visits Elizabeth. She brings a freshly steamed lobster tail, a request from her niece. Elizabeth beams when she sees Sarah, and cheers when her aunt puts the fresh lobster and some melted butter on a plate. My sister and I are amazed when Elizabeth picks up her knife and fork and, mouthful by mouthful, eats the entire seafood meal! She hasn't eaten, let alone savored, a meal like this since early last summer.

Sarah will be spending the night, and I go down the hall to get the sheets, pillowcases, and a towel, and then I extend the chair by the window and make her bed. After I kiss my daughter good night and slowly walk out of the room, I hear them talking about which movie they will watch tonight. I'm reminded of the overnights that my girls enjoyed at their aunt's house and how they all lined up in her king-sized bed eating popcorn and watching movies. I smile knowing that, despite this very different setting, they will have as good a night as possible together.

Several days later, after Elizabeth returns home, my parents ask if we'd like to spend the week at their house on Cape Cod. We all want the change of scene. Olivia's teachers are very supportive of her taking the week off to be with her sister and grandparents. Susie's husband, Peter, drives us there. Elizabeth and I sleep upstairs in a large dormered room with twin beds. Olivia sleeps in the guest bedroom downstairs. Both bedrooms look out at a freshwater kettle-hole pond, and cool breezes waft into our rooms at night.

Since my girls were infants, my parents have showered them with affection. Even as a toddler, Olivia loved having solo overnights with her Nana and Grampa, who lived two hours away. Most children her age would be reluctant to leave their parents, but not Olivia, who had often asked Nana, "Can I come and stay?" Olivia loved going to the hair salon with my mother and chatting with everyone. She also loved going with her Nana to get her nails done. She had her first manicure at age two! While Olivia bonded tightly with my mom, Elizabeth bonded with my father, referring to him as "Shampy." This melted his heart.

My parents moved from Connecticut to Cape Cod when my girls were in first grade and kindergarten. They moved into a spacious, traditional Cape shingle-sided house with a large yard and a freshwater pond, and they were only a few minutes from the beach. Olivia and Elizabeth enjoyed many weekends together with their grandparents, especially during the summer, when they spent endless hours playing on the beach and swimming in the sea.

During this visit, my mother makes an extra effort to take care of Olivia, and my father, a retired internist, focuses on Elizabeth. Mom takes Olivia shopping for school clothes and to have a manicure. They bring back the soft cotton T-shirts and pajama pants from Victoria's Secret that Elizabeth has asked for and a bundle of fashion magazines. In the late afternoons, Mom and my girls flip through magazines, watch TV, and snooze in my parents' king-sized bed.

Dad regularly asks Elizabeth how she feels and if he can do anything to make her more comfortable. He fluffs up her pillows and buys her favorite food at the grocery store. He wraps her aching knee in Ace bandages, checks her pulse, and listens to her heartbeat. In his steadfast ways, he brings comfort and a sense of calm to his grand-daughter and, in fact, to all of us.

In the evenings, Dad and I make dinner and talk quietly. I can ask my father difficult medical questions, reassured he is not only a physician but also one who loves Elizabeth as only a grandparent can.

"When will she be able to gain some of her strength back?" I ask.

"I don't know, Faith. Her immune system is very suppressed, and chemotherapy treatments stop all of the body's quickly multiplying cells, not only the cancerous ones. These treatments are extremely harsh on her body and make her exhausted."

"And what exactly will the doctors learn from the next CT scan?"

"They'll be able to see if tumors are growing in other areas besides her knee, like they did when they scanned her lungs."

I press him, "Dad, you mean she really could have tumors in other places?"

"Yes, her cancer has metastasized," he says gently. "I'm so sorry, Faith."

Around midnight on the first night of our visit, Elizabeth begins to vomit without stopping. I wake my father, and we call a nurse, who agrees that Dad should give Elizabeth an injection of anti-nau-sea medication. Soon her retching ends and she falls back asleep. As I lie in bed next to her, I feel a deep sense of relief. I feel utterly alone caring for Elizabeth at home, but here my dad gives me the support that I yearn to have in my marriage. Exhausted, I fall into a deep sleep.

Chapter 6

A Door Closes;
A Window Opens

Early October 2000

After we return from the Cape, the tension in our house escalates. At breakfast one morning, Neville complains, "You're never home. I have to do all the work. I don't have time to shop, take care of the housework, and do my job to pay the bills."

I'm furious. "What do you think I've been doing all these weeks at the hospital? Do you really think we can drop Elizabeth off and let the doctors and nurses care for her as if she doesn't have a family? What are you thinking? It's not all about how this impacts you!"

Elizabeth hears our raised voices, and she calls for me from her bedroom. I go to her, and she asks, "What's wrong, Mommy?"

"I'm having a disagreement with your dad." She gazes steadily at me, guessing at our quarrel.

Later, after I've given her breakfast and her morning medications, she settles in for a nap.

"Will you be okay if I go for a walk, honey?" I ask.

"Sure. Have a good walk, Mommy."

I don't see Neville in the kitchen, but I hear him on the phone downstairs in his studio. I leave without speaking to him and head out for my walk. Soon I reach the conservation path that leads through a lightly wooded forest to a pond. Walking along the path, I breathe deeply, and with each breath my anger lessens. I pause and sit on a log bathed in sunlight, feeling calmer. Suddenly, to my surprise and as if someone next to me had spoken, I hear, *It's time to leave him, Faith.* And in that moment I *know*; this is the only way I can save Elizabeth, Olivia, and me.

I stand up and begin to walk back home. I feel calm and focused. My girls and I will no longer have to bear the unbearable at home. It's over. It's done.

After Olivia comes home from school and is sitting with Elizabeth, I tell them I need to go out for a while. I drive to church to speak with my minister. My decision tumbles out of me.

"I need to leave my home. It's no longer tolerable to live with my husband. I have to focus solely on my girls now."

My minister says, "I agree. I've seen the stress in your family, and now you have to save yourself and your children."

But the weight of this decision is overwhelming. I start to cry and say, "But how can I do this? I only have ten thousand dollars to my name, Elizabeth will have treatments for a year, and Olivia is totally overwhelmed already. How can I afford to rent a condo or an apartment and look after both my daughters?"

She reaches out, holds my hand, and calmly says, "When a door closes, a window will open."

That evening, I call Lisa and tell her that I have to move out, that Neville is unbearable to live with any longer. Without a moment's hesitation, she says, "You can live in my summer house in Sherborn, rent-free, of course."

I dissolve into tears and say, "Thank you. Thank you. I'll let you know soon if this will work well for us."

A moment later I call my sister Susie, who in a heartbeat says, "Come and live with me."

After speaking with my girls, they say, "Let's go live with Susie."

Chapter 7

Flight

Mid-October 2000

I'm sleepless with worry about leaving my home and my marriage and beginning a new life as a single parent, but I move forward. I ask Susie and my friend Beth if they will help us move out while Neville is away over Columbus Day weekend. They arrive early on the agreed-upon day. Olivia helps Elizabeth into Susie's van, and together we load their bags of clothes. Beth fills her car with what Olivia needs for school and sundries they want to bring. I gather all Elizabeth's medicines and medical equipment and my clothing. Shaking, I drop a note on the front hall table, close and lock the front door, and drive away.

When we get to Susie's house, Olivia helps Elizabeth walk slowly up the back staircase to our new home. I bring our suitcases into the bedroom that Elizabeth and I will share above the garage. The room gets ample sunlight, with two windows at either end as well as two dormered windows. Twin beds are tucked on opposite sides of this cozy room, with a night table standing between. A comfortable chair and lamp sit under the dormered windows. Olivia's bedroom is separated from ours by a short hallway and bathroom. She will stay in her cousin Jon's bedroom. Seven-year-old Jon is excited to "move" and set up his cot in his parents' walk-in closet. His older siblings—Robin, age thirteen, and Dave, age twelve—have their own bedrooms.

After we tour the rooms, Susie hugs me and promises to do all that she can to help and harbor us safely.

Several weeks later, after we've settled into Susie's house, my cousin Julia announces that she is coming to visit and help us for a week. Her friends will take care of her three middle-school-aged children during the day, and David, Julia's husband, will take care of them at night.

Julia and I bonded when we were very young. She grew up in a family filled with the laughter and antics of seven children born within eleven years. As a frequent overnight guest at Julia's house, I loved listening to the sounds of commotion on Saturday mornings; peeking in the refrigerator piled high with food; and being amazed at the sight of nine pairs of downhill skis, boots, parkas, snow pants, and mountains of hats, gloves, and woolen ski socks in their mud room. Quite a contrast to the orderly quiet of three well-behaved girls in the home where I grew up!

My connection to Julia grew stronger when she and I attended the same boarding school. She was a freshman and I was a first-year junior. Being a day student and not knowing my classmates yet, I frequented Julia's dorm room during the fifteen-minute break after lunch or during a free period. We played endless card games, our favorites being War, Gin Rummy 500, Spit!, and Old Maid.

Soon after college, Julia married David, a handsome and kind Brit. They moved to England for several years and then settled in New Jersey. When our children were young, we often saw each other at our grandmother's house in Connecticut or when Julia and her family stayed with us in Massachusetts. Long phone calls kept us connected between visits.

By the time Julia arrives at my sister's house in late October, I've lost twenty-five pounds in six weeks and am struggling to sleep. My concentration is so poor that I can't even drive. I am so grateful when she arrives to help me.

On the first day, Julia drives me to the hospital to be with Elizabeth, who is nearing the end of a five-day hospital stay after receiving her third round of chemotherapy. Even in her weakened state, Elizabeth gives Julia a radiant smile. Always upbeat, Julia soon has us laughing as she relays with humor her stories about being in military-style hospitals in England with nurses who ran their floors like commanding officers. She regales us with almost unbelievable but true hospital tales, and we laugh for the first time in months. Olivia enjoys spending special time with Julia, who drives her to the mall to shop for clothes and to appointments after school. Julia gives our entire family a big lift.

Chapter 8
Heartache
November 2000

The relentless march of treatments carries on, leaving Elizabeth frail and exhausted. She weighs 110 pounds, far too little for her five foot nine frame. I'm aware that Olivia is withdrawing from me, which is worrying. Although she is being well cared for, at this point it is not mainly by me. Every morning, Susie drives Olivia twelve miles to her high school in Sudbury. Various friends pick her up at the end of the school day and drive her back to our "home" in Wellesley. In the evenings I ask Olivia how her day was, and she replies only with "Fine." So I pursue her.

"Well, what made your day okay? Did you like your French class? Did you like discussing Shakespeare in your English class?"

"You know I like my French teacher. She's the best. English class was just okay."

One evening I try again to engage her in conversation. "After you finish your homework, can you come upstairs and watch TV with Elizabeth? She knows that you have your schoolwork to do, but she misses you."

Olivia gives me a cursory glance. "Yes."

As she frequently does, she goes downstairs to study with Robin in the basement office. I know little about her days at school and new friendships, but when I look into her soulful eyes and see her frightened expressions, I know she is torn up about her sister's frail state. I'm at a loss. She won't let me in to comfort her.

Even though so much of Olivia's life has spun out of control, she keeps control over her student life. She focuses on her work and excels, usually getting As. She knows how much I value education, and I'm certain part of her effort is to win my approval.

In the second week of November, Elizabeth returns to the hospital for her fourth round of chemotherapy. The doctors warn us that the combination of methotrexate, ifosfamide, VP16, and cisplatin is going to be the harshest treatment so far. We brace for the worst. It hits on the third day, when Elizabeth begins throwing up violently. The nurses give her IVs with anti-nausea medication and to replace the fluids she lost. We had hoped to return home before the weekend, but Elizabeth's cell counts are abysmal. After hearing she has to stay longer, Elizabeth sobs, and my heart sinks. I'm desperate to lift her spirits and to somehow create a special night.

First, I suggest that we watch a movie, and she likes this idea. While she and a social worker pick through various movies, I walk to Antonio's, an Italian restaurant I discovered a few weeks ago. I bring back an order of fresh tortellini, which Elizabeth enjoys with ginger ale. Then I pop in the video, *My Best Friend's Wedding*. We prop ourselves up with pillows and soon are laughing and singing along with the movie. Feeling stronger for the first time in days, Elizabeth wraps her arms around my neck. "I love you, Mommy."

"I love you too, honey, and will be by your side all night."

Despite Elizabeth's intense struggles, we have two occasions to celebrate over the next few weeks. First, the scan of Elizabeth's lungs shows that the tumors have dramatically reduced in size, and some seem even to have disappeared. We are elated! For the first time since her diagnosis, she has received good news. It boosts Elizabeth's, Olivia's, and my spirits immensely.

Our second cause for celebration is on November 16, when Lisa gives birth to healthy twin boys. Several weeks later, when she visits us at my sister's house, Olivia, Elizabeth, Susie, and I take turns holding her sons, Peter and Nathaniel. Their warmth radiates to my skin, and their intent gazes stir up hope in me with the promise of new life. I could have held them for hours, stroking their soft tufts of hair and looking with amazement at their newborn faces and their tiny hands and feet. A few moments later, Lisa sits next to me and asks, "Will you be Nathaniel's godmother?"

With tears of joy streaming down my face, I say, "Yes."

Chapter 9

Sorrow and Joy

December 2000

B y early winter, I begin to feel a connectedness with my women friends, whose comfort and presence ease the ache of my loneliness and my fear of the unknown.

One of these friends is Diana. In 1993, six months after we moved to Lincoln, I was asked to join the town of Lincoln's tennis team. During the first practice of the "A" team, when I met eight spunky athletic women, I was particularly drawn to Diana. From the first time we met on opposite sides of the net, Diana radiated goodwill and kindness. She laughed when she missed an easy overhead and congratulated partners and opponents alike. Within days of our meeting, Diana offered to show me around town and introduce me to many of her friends.

Several months later, Diana invited my family over for dinner. To this day, I remember the mouthwatering aromas of beef roasting in the oven, gravy bubbling in a pot, and green beans steaming on the stovetop. Olivia's and Elizabeth's eyes opened wide when Diana showed them her homemade mint-chip ice cream pie and the creamy chocolate sauce warming on the stove top. After dinner, while the adults chatted in the living room, Diana gave my girls crayons and coloring books, and board games to play. This memorable dinner became the first of literally dozens of meals I've savored at Diana's table over the past ten years.

Also, during my first year in Lincoln, and with Diana's help and encouragement, I decided to change careers and become a real estate broker. Diana had been a broker in town for fifteen years and became a mentor to me. In my first year I had almost no business, but in the second year, Diana let me cover for her when she was on vacation, and soon she was sharing listings with me. This was the beginning of a successful career and business relationship.

Diana never stopped being generous with her help. One summer when two teenage sons of French friends were visiting us, my finances were tight, so day trips were all I could afford. For the first few days, we visited nearby state parks and took walking tours of historic sites in Boston. Then to my great surprise, Diana invited my family and our French guests to stay with her on Martha's Vineyard. We had never been there and were excited to see its renowned beaches, quaint seaside houses, and natural beauty. We took her up on her invitation later that summer. Diana greeted us at the Vineyard Haven ferry dock, and we began a memorable four-day visit that included picnics on beaches that stretched for miles, swimming in currents that swept us along in the sea, and fresh seafood dinners with Diana's family and friends.

Now, four years later, Diana continues her tireless efforts to help me. She drives Olivia where she needs to go, delivers meals to Susie's house, and serves as the bookkeeper for the fund set up by my church community to help pay our uncovered medical costs. She even stays with Elizabeth in the hospital almost every Friday night, giving me the chance to catch up on needed sleep.

Diana does much more than give me times off to rest. During this stressful time, I have been eating less and less and have lost a great deal of weight. My emotional state has deteriorated too. One night when the girls are at Susie's, I feel swamped with terror about possibly losing Elizabeth and the fear that I don't have the forti-tude needed to care for both my daughters in the coming months. Overwhelmed by despair and desperation, I drive to Diana's house, weeping, and collapse in weakness on her doorstep. She opens the door, lifts me up, hugs me, and tells me to lie down in her guest room. She brings me tea and toast, and she stays by my side until my keening wails cease.

As the weeks go by, I begin to realize that no matter how much support I get from Diana, my sisters, and close friends, I still have to cope with the ongoing nightmare of what's happening. The strain on Elizabeth, Olivia, and me almost reaches a breaking point during Elizabeth's fifth round of chemotherapy. While expectations of a joyful Christmas abound outside us, and people are getting ready for parties and family gatherings, we are overwhelmed by fear of our unknown future.

In early December, it's time to return to the hospital. My youngest and I drive past storefronts decorated with gifts and window displays filled with lights, cars with Christmas trees tied to their roofs, and lampposts adorned with evergreens. When we arrive at the hospital, I help Elizabeth into a wheelchair and leave her in the front lobby with her overnight bag, her favorite purple fleece blanket, and a soft, downy pillow. A volunteer stays with her while I search for a parking spot in the jammed garage. After locking the car, I grab my overnight bag, enter the lobby, and wheel Elizabeth up to the pediatric floor. The doctors and nurses greet us with warmth and kindness. We settle in to our assigned room as we have done so many times before.

The first night as I lie awake watching cisplatin drip, drip, drip into my child's port, tears stream down my face. *Why, God? Why, God, is my daughter bulleted with invasive growths? Why, God? Can't You make her well again? She should be back on the soccer field, fear-lessly blocking the ball that's speeding toward the goal. She should be swimming the backstroke effortlessly during her Saturday morning meets. She should be spending overnights with friends or cuddling with Olivia while watching TV.*

Why, God, does my beloved younger daughter have to suffer so? And can't You save Olivia from the terror that she might lose her sister, her best friend, her confidante—the one who makes her laugh and laugh with her sidesplitting silly acts. The one whose bounciness brought levity to the oppressive feeling in our house.

Instead, here my child is in ragged condition after five grueling days of back-to-back intense chemotherapy. On the sixth day, we receive the "all clear" to return home. The twelve-mile ride back to Wellesley seems like an eternity, but once home, Elizabeth is safely tucked into bed and falls into a deep sleep.

The following seven days are the harshest yet for her. Elizabeth does not even have the strength to walk the ten steps to the bathroom, so I place a portable commode by her bedside. I offer her a spoonful of applesauce, but she's too weak to swallow. She only sips small amounts of water and ginger ale. The worst for me comes one afternoon when she wakes from a nap. She looks intently into my eyes, saying nothing. Her gaze conveys the unbearable message that she knows she may not survive. Up until this moment, she and I had not acknowledged this possibility. After a few minutes of silence, without giving voice to her fear, Elizabeth says, "Mommy, I want you to be happy. Remarry one day. And be with children. Do you remember how the children loved you when you read to them in my first grade?"

The ups and downs of our roller-coaster ride continue. Christmas is now only ten days away. My parents, wanting to give us a special holiday, invite us to spend Christmas Eve at the Four Seasons in Boston, a luxury that we could only dream of. My girls are over the moon with excitement, which helps Elizabeth regain some strength. On the afternoon of Christmas Eve, my parents pick us up and drive us to Boston.

We are standing in the front lobby, looking in awe at the festive decorations. Dad speaks to the hotel manager and turns to us. "Our rooms aren't ready yet, so they'd like us to stay in different rooms." The hotel manager leads us to the top floor and opens the door to our room, a vast suite decorated with floral arrangements, a fully orna-mented Christmas tree, and a teddy bear the size of a cub sitting on the sofa. Elizabeth immediately hobbles over and picks up the bear and holds it tightly. Our eyes fill with tears.

After we settle into the presidential suite, high tea appears, with scones, butter, and jam and a surprise gift of chocolate-covered strawberries from Molly and her daughter, Annie, one of Elizabeth's best friends. This is a dream come true—a magical Christmas for my girls.

Early on Christmas morning, I first greet my parents, who are placing gifts under the Christmas tree. I find Elizabeth in front of elegant mirrors in the bathroom putting on makeup and her nat-ural-hair wig. She hugs me and then hobbles into the bedroom to waken Olivia. "It's Christmas, Olivia! Wake up!" We enjoy a delicious breakfast of fruit, muffins and croissants, scrambled eggs, orange juice, and tea in our suite. Outside, the trees in the Boston Garden sparkle with white lights; people are walking briskly along the snowy paths. We open presents, share memories, and cuddle on the sofa or in Nana and Grampy's big bed. For twenty-four hours, it's as though Elizabeth, Olivia, and I are living a fairytale filled with gifts of love and joy.

Later in the afternoon, as we are packing to leave, Elizabeth tells me that her back is sore and aches. My father lifts her shirt and dis-covers that she has shingles on her back. Tears fill her eyes. I call her doctor and tell him that Elizabeth desperately does not want to be admitted to the hospital this evening. Dr. Kin explains to me how serious it is that Elizabeth has shingles. If she has them on her back, he says, she likely has them on some of her internal organs as well. But because it is Christmas Day, he agrees to let us go home if we keep Elizabeth quarantined in her room. He orders a prescription to be taken immediately. If her pain increases during the night, he insists that she has to be admitted.

After being blessed with twenty-four hours of happiness, I cry out silently, *Why, God, why does it have to end this way?*

Chapter 10

Grace

January 2001

Despite her pain and discouragement, Elizabeth finds new meaning when she is in the hospital for her sixth round of chemotherapy. On the rare occasions when she feels strong enough, she decides on her own to visit the young patients on her floor. I discover this one afternoon when, to my surprise, she says, "I'll be back soon," and wheels herself out of the room. I peek down the hall and see her pull the hood of her sweatshirt over her bald head, knock on a door, and roll herself into the room of a new patient. I imagine her gentle manner and engaging smile as she talks to a stricken and frightened child. A few minutes later, I hear her say, "See you soon," and then knock on another door. "Hi, I'm Elizabeth. Can I come in?"

At first, I'm stunned that Elizabeth is using her meager reservoir of strength to comfort others, but soon understand that she connects with the plight of these young patients. She knows their fear. Even in the midst of horrendous cancer treatments, the teenage Elizabeth is shedding her self-consciousness, leaving her safety zone, and reaching out to others. She is becoming a young woman. Her actions embrace what a minister once told me: "Compassion, at its core, is about suffering, suffering with another. . . ."

The social workers, nurses, and doctors take notice of Elizabeth's new behavior too. When one social worker remarks to her how much she has helped a child who is terribly afraid, Elizabeth smiles modestly. One afternoon, a nurse taps me on the shoulder and says, "Elizabeth is amazing. She explains medical procedures to children in a way that they can understand. She's becoming the 'greeter' for the floor; she even welcomes kids' difficult questions."

One morning, the mother of a patient with the same diagnosis as Elizabeth walks up to me in tears. She says, "During our first night when I was sitting by my daughter's bedside, Elizabeth visited. We've been so scared about her cancer and our unknown future. But your daughter's smile, warmth, and kindness gave us our first feelings of hope."

How can Elizabeth summon this courage and strength? The only possible answer for me is *with God's grace.*

During this hospitalization, I've been invited to be present at a medical conference call attended by the Massachusetts commissioner of health, a Harvard public-health policy expert, a visiting specialist, and Dr. Kin. They are discussing the pros and cons of offering Elizabeth an experimental treatment that has been used only twenty times and only at a hospital in the Midwest. I am scared about the meeting but need to be there. I don't want Elizabeth's case to remain an anonymous number.

The medical professionals review the merits of the experimental treatment. During clinical trials, doctors found that this infusion stopped the growth of bone tumors by cutting off their blood supply, which is their lifeline. It also relieved patients' pain considerably. Although the long-term benefits are not known, this treatment looks to me like a candle burning brightly on a moonless night.

With the uncertainties about the treatment and the discovery that her health insurance provider might refuse to cover the nearly $50,000 costs, I'm swamped by anxiety. After an hour, they reach their conclusion: Dr. Kin and medical specialists will give Elizabeth the treatment, and the Harvard public-health policy expert will campaign for the insurance coverage. I can barely control my immeasurable relief when I hear their decision. Only a few moments later it occurs to me to ask, "What will be the primary benefit for my daughter?"

The doctor's response, "It will be palliative," wipes away my relief, leaving heartbreak and rage.

I want to explode. Palliative care? Only to relieve her pain but not to cure her? I silently scream, *Can't anyone, anyone, anyone or any treatment save my child?* But I don't explode. These professionals are working so hard to bring this experimental treatment to Boston just for Elizabeth's benefit. I swallow my anger wrapped in a toxic coating of fear.

I look at each person around the conference table and, in a whisper, say, "I am very grateful to each of you for your concern, professional guidance, and advocacy." As I leave the room, I pray they don't see me shaking.

Chapter 11

Blindsided

February 2001

E lizabeth's doctors have to harvest and freeze some of her own stem cells in preparation for the upcoming experimental treatment. Following the infusion, Elizabeth will need a transfusion of her own harvested stem cells to help her body recover. At this trying time, to my great relief, Julia arrives to help us for one more week.

On the day after Julia arrives, I wake at five thirty to give Elizabeth her morning medications, injections, and some breakfast in order for her to be ready for what looks like a long day ahead. We leave Susie's house at six forty-five, and Julia drives us to the hospital. We spend the morning in an oncology and hematology clinic, where nurses draw blood to make sure that Elizabeth's cell counts are adequate before starting the procedure to harvest stem cells. Elizabeth, lying on a hospital bed, is fretful and holds my hand for comfort. Julia speaks softly to us as the hours crawl by. Just before noon, the oncology doctors tell us that Elizabeth's counts are too low, and they cannot safely harvest her stem cells today. As she sits up, her head droops as she resigns herself to this disappointing outcome. During the ride home, Julia tries to keep our spirits up as she tells us about the antics of her three young children. Later that afternoon, I receive a call; the doctors urge us to return tomorrow. We all know that

Elizabeth's tumors are multiplying, and chemotherapy is no longer effective. It's critical that she have this experimental treatment right away.

Early on Tuesday morning, we repeat the same process, only it is more grueling for Elizabeth, who is weaker than the day before. So, this morning we push on—Julia strong and me trying to be—and my child agrees to more tests. As we wait in the clinic to learn of the cell count results, Elizabeth looks imploringly at me. Her penetrating gaze tells me that she is fully aware of the gravity of the situation. As the morning hours drag on, she clings to my arm, willing the results to be positive. The doctors return with grave faces. We drive home in silence. In the afternoon, Julia takes Olivia shopping, and when my daughter returns, she proudly shows me her new clothes. That evening the doctors call again but tell us to stay home tomorrow to give Elizabeth a day to rest, eat, and gain some strength.

On Thursday at six forty-five, Julia drives us back to the hospital. Silently, I check my hope at the curb. In the clinic, Elizabeth is pale and drawn. The doctors draw blood at eight fifteen. At eleven forty-five, Elizabeth reaches for my hand when the doctors walk toward us. They say, "We can proceed to draw your stem cells today." Julia shouts out, "Yahoo!" Soon, tubes are connected to Elizabeth's port. Moments later, released from the built-up tension, she falls asleep. Three hours later, I push Elizabeth, who is humped over with exhaustion in her wheelchair, down a labyrinth of corridors to Julia, who is waiting in our car. Julia's help and emotional strength propels Olivia, Elizabeth, and me through a perilous week. I wouldn't have had the endurance to do this alone.

During this frightening time, I am also comforted by the support of my stalwart friend Beth and my sisters. I first met Beth on the tennis courts seven years ago, and she has been my athletic partner since then. Every week during the warm weather months, we play singles tennis or partner in doubles. When facing intimidating players on the opposite side of the court, Beth, in an assertive voice, says to me, "We are big, strong women!" She stirs up my inner strength and taps into my competitive spirit. We have had many epic three-set battles, almost always ending in victory.

Beth brings that strength into her professional life as a nurse practitioner too. In the fall of 2000 and the winter of 2001, she works at a medical clinic in addition to working as a nurse at a women's college. On Friday mornings, during her free half day, she visits me in Wellesley. Some days she gives me a massage, but mainly we go for walks. I talk about Elizabeth's recent test results, and Beth explains medical terminology to me in a way that I can understand. Sometimes we stop and sit on a stone wall while I sob and sob. Other times, I simply can't talk, my suffering extinguishing my words. But somehow, after each visit with Beth, I'm able to summon up some reserves of strength.

One morning we meet at an indoor pool in Sudbury. We swim the breaststroke side by side while talking. Beth offers a proposal: She has spoken with my friend Lisa about our long-hoped-for home of our own. One where we can blossom as a family. Because they know I can't afford it, four or five of my friends want to lend me the down payment. They say I can cover my mortgage payments when I return to my real estate career. And when I sell my house in Lincoln, I can repay their loan.

Not only does this offer reflect their generosity, but it demonstrates to me how much they love me and my girls. They recognize that we need and deserve a safe and happy home. By the end of our swim, I've agreed to this proposal. Several weeks later, Beth calls me and says, "You can begin looking for a new house, Faith!"

The timing of this offer couldn't have been better. Susie and her family have been sheltering and caring for us for the past five months.

I know that Susie is exhausted, and I'm worried that she's stretched to her limit.

In the meantime, Susie continues to drive Olivia to high school each morning, does the grocery shopping, plans meals, and sits with Elizabeth when I want to take a walk or visit a friend. Susie never wavers in her support, especially when we face frightening events. One morning, Elizabeth has a nosebleed that won't stop, and within the hour, she is vomiting blood every few minutes. While Susie holds a bucket under my youngest's chin, I call Dr. Kin. He wants us to get to the hospital immediately. Susie and I try and fail to carry Elizabeth to the car. While I call for an ambulance, Susie calls a neighbor, and within minutes he carries Elizabeth, limp with exhaustion and blood loss, into the waiting ambulance. Susie and I climb into the back, and the EMTs give Elizabeth an injection of anti-nausea medication that makes her feel less queasy. Her nosebleed rages on.

At the hospital, the doctors give Elizabeth more anti-nausea medication and put in an order for platelets. They tell us that her cell counts are so low that her blood loss will continue until her platelet count is higher. While I hold cool cloths on Elizabeth's forehead, Susie sits quietly with us. After an hour of waiting, the first transfusion of platelets begins. Thirty minutes later, Elizabeth is still bleeding but at a slower rate. Looking concerned, the medical team begins a second transfusion of platelets. As the transfusion drips, drips, drips into my daughter's port, I silently pray for the horror of this day to end. By the early afternoon, the bleeding ceases, to our great relief. This episode has left Elizabeth ravaged.

But before we leave, Neville shows up at the hospital. Somebody on the hospital staff must have called him, not knowing that my girls no longer want to see him. I'm speechless with fury but don't want to show my anger in front of Elizabeth. She's been through enough today.

He stands at the opening in the curtain drawn around Elizabeth, Susie, and me. Susie quietly leaves and summons hospital staff, who move nearby. Neville asks, "Can I see you alone, without your mother, Elizabeth?"

"Will you stay close, Mommy?"

"Yes."

She nods. He walks to her and whispers to her. I stand about fifteen feet away and can't hear their conversation. After a few minutes pass, he walks out, glares at me aggressively, and says, "She wants me to leave. You've ruined my relationship with her."

The next day, after I tell my older sister, Sarah, about this horrific day, she ramps up her efforts to help too. She's the business manager for a large urban church in the midst of a capital campaign, and she works ten-hour days. It's been difficult for her to help out because she is stretched to her max. But today she jumps in and asks, "How can I help the most?"

"Can you spend time with Olivia?" I ask. "I'm worried about her. We've lost the close connection that we rekindled over Christmas. Now she barely speaks to me in the evenings. I know she is suffering terribly seeing her little sister get weaker and weaker. And she recently blurted that she's angry with me for not leaving her father sooner."

Sarah responds, "I'm sorry, Faith. She's had so many difficult changes, not to mention that she's at a new high school and is learning how to fit in, get good grades, and make new friends. Of course, I'll spend more time with her."

My daughters have always adored Sarah. When they were preschoolers and Sarah arrived for a visit, they'd jump up and down and shout, "YaYa's coming! YaYa's here!" Unable to pronounce *Sarah* when they were toddlers, Sarah morphed into "YaYa," which has remained the children's nickname for her ever since. She's been present at every birthday celebration, family holiday, and school play. Now, I'm praying that she can reach Olivia, help her cope with the challenges she's facing, and even bring some fun into her life.

Soon, Sarah is taking Olivia shopping, playing board games, or inviting her for overnights on the weekends. Olivia invites Elizabeth to join their overnight forays whenever she feels up to it. After spending time with her aunt, Olivia has a bounce in her step for the first time in months.

Chapter 12

A Respite
March 2001

Elizabeth has her seventh round of chemotherapy, but this treatment is not as harsh because she needs to be strong enough to receive the experimental infusion in April. By mid-March, we find out that, for the first time since her treatments began, she is allowed to travel. My parents seize this opportunity and invite the three of us to visit them in Naples, Florida. The day before we leave, the doctors do one more round of blood tests to make sure she's okay. We're elated when we receive the green light.

The flight is difficult for Elizabeth, not only because she is five foot nine but because her right knee has swollen to the size of a small bowling ball due to the growth of her primary tumor. The flight attendant sees how uncomfortable Elizabeth is and moves her to a different section with greater legroom. When we arrive at my parents' condominium after the seven-hour door-to-door trip, she falls exhausted into bed.

The following day, she wakes up next to Olivia, who is sleeping in the twin bed near her. Before Elizabeth's diagnosis, she and her sister were very close and spent endless hours together riding on the school bus, playing at recess, having overnights with friends, and even playing with their hamsters. Now, for the first time since Elizabeth's diagnosis, they get to sleep in the same room, watch TV, chat, look at magazines, share the joy of warm weather, and sit in the sun, something they've always loved to do together.

After breakfast, Olivia and I can see that Elizabeth is very weak and wants to return to bed, but we don't want her to be left out. We make up a cot and roll it into the living room, where we're all sitting. She settles in, and as we chat, she drifts off to sleep. When she wakes up, Elizabeth says, "Nana, I'm so happy to be here where it's sunny and warm, and I'm so glad that I don't have to go to the hospital for a whole week!" My mother smiles and squeezes Elizabeth's hand.

Olivia leaves her weekday routine behind too. The first day she's quiet with fatigue, but by that night, as the girls settle into bed, laughter fills their room. For the first time in months, I fall asleep contentedly, listening to my girls chatting in the room next to mine.

After a few days of rest, Nana takes the girls shopping in an outdoor mall. Elizabeth is feeling stronger, and walking with her crutches, she can keep up. Olivia looks happy too, being able to share this outing with her sister, something they've always loved to do with their Nana.

One morning, my girls and I ride a tram on a wooden bridge that meanders through mangroves and swamps filled with tropical birds, verdant flora, and alligators! We arrive at our destination, a bright-white sandy beach that leads to a celadon-green sea. We inhale the familiar, moist, salty air. We support Elizabeth, who is walking with a step-hop, step-hop gait down the handicap ramp to the beach.

Even with our support, when we reach the sand, Elizabeth's hopping is difficult and painful for her. She's determined to reach the water, so Olivia and I do our best to help her. She scuffles forward, and when the cool waters splash over her feet, she sighs.

It's high season at the beach, and vacationers are sitting on every available chaise lounge and beach chair. We can't find a place for Elizabeth to sit, and she cannot stand much longer. We are about to give up when I feel a tap on my shoulder. I turn to see a woman in her midforties smiling at me. "You can have our chaise lounges. We can sit on our towels."

I look to where she's pointing and see that she also has a teenage daughter. Moments later, I watch the woman support her Down syndrome daughter as she struggles to stand up. Of all of the hundreds of children, teenagers, and adults on the beach, they are the ones who help us.

Chapter 13
Worth the Risks
April 2001

On the morning before we leave for Elizabeth's experimental treatment, she's singing "My Favorite Things" from *The Sound of Music*. In an upbeat voice, she mentions several things she wants me to put in her overnight bag. I've already added in a few of her favorite things: a purple fleece blanket, a soft small pillow, her favorite toy—a well-worn brown stuffed dog named Mutsy—her makeup kit, several Victoria's Secret long-sleeved tops and matching pajama pants, and teen magazines. My heart feels lighter hearing her happiness this morning.

At the hospital, Elizabeth is greeted by the attending doctors and nurses. We thought that she'd have a room in pediatrics, but they bring her to a private room on the top floor. Dr. Kin smiles at Elizabeth and reviews the upcoming procedure. "You'll be in this room in isolation for three days. As we discussed before, you'll be given an infusion through your port. Because it contains a radioactive material, the doctors who set up your IV will be covered in protective clothing from head to toe. They may look like astronauts walking on the moon!"

Elizabeth smiles.

"Several hours after you receive this infusion, a doctor in protective clothing will return and flush your lines. You'll be here for three days on your own, but, of course, someone will also bring you food and drinks. After three days, your mom will pick you up, and you'll be able to return home."

"Will it hurt or will I throw up?" she asks.

"No, it should be painless and shouldn't cause any nausea."

"Can I make phone calls?"

"Of course!"

She takes a breath and says, "Well, I'm ready."

Elizabeth looks at me for a moment and then turns back to Dr. Kin. "Even if it doesn't save me, I hope it will help save others who have my cancer."

I don't want her to see that her courage and awareness have just knocked the breath out of me. I kiss my child and wave good-bye from the doorway.

After I have a sleepless night, Elizabeth calls me. She sounds weary but says, "It wasn't bad, really. I'm not hungry, that's all, and I can't wait to come home. I'm calling Olivia and Robin and all of my friends. The nurses said that I can use the hospital's phone as much as I like."

"I'm so proud of you, and it sounds like you're doing well. In two more days, I'll pick you up! Would you like to invite a friend over after you're back home?"

"Yes!"

When she recovers, Elizabeth, Olivia, and I begin our house-hunting adventure. We start on the internet, printing off several listings and checking off or circling the ones we want to learn more about. We focus on condominiums in Lincoln and houses in Sudbury. We're elated that our dream to have a home of our own is becoming a reality.

While Olivia is in school, Elizabeth and I drive by several houses on our list. We are intrigued by two houses, and at Elizabeth's insistence, I call the listing brokers from the car. Soon we have entrée into both houses. The first is close to Sudbury Middle School, and Elizabeth likes the idea of having friends walk over after school. Once inside, she enthusiastically proceeds to tell me which bedroom would be hers, Olivia's, and mine. She practically has us moved in! But before we make any decisions, I want to see the other possibility, which is in a central location on a quiet cul-de-sac.

The moment I walk into the house, I know it is the one. The living and dining rooms have an open layout and shimmer with sunlight. At the back of the house, sliding doors lead to a deck, a gravel patio, and a sweeping view of the lawn and woodlands. I hold my breath as Elizabeth walks around the house.

"Come here quickly, Mommy!"

I go downstairs, where she's standing in an unfinished wood-paneled room about twenty by forty feet.

"Can we make this into Olivia's and my room, where we can have friends over? Can we have a sofa and a TV?"

I imagine the room with carpeting and fresh paint. "Of course you can."

It's two forty-five and time to pick up Olivia from high school. She's standing in the bright sunlight talking with friends. Elizabeth asks, "Can you get my crutches for me, so I can go talk with Olivia's friends?"

"Sure, I can."

Olivia runs over and leads her sister to her friends. A wave of happiness passes through me seeing Elizabeth chatting with students, enjoying an everyday activity. Ten minutes later, both girls climb into my Volvo. Elizabeth is just about to burst as she describes the house we both like. Once again, the owner lets us in, and Olivia surveys each room. She asks, "Mommy, can we make the downstairs into two rooms instead of one? I'd like my bedroom downstairs, and we can have a family room for Liz and me too."

"Yes, if Elizabeth agrees."

That evening I write an offer to purchase this house. I already know how much my friends will lend me for the down payment, and I've calculated what the mortgage payments and taxes will be. It's a stretch, but it feels right. Susie is anxious that I'm making this decision too quickly. She wants to see the house and accompany me when I present the offer to the selling agent and the owners. Susie and I drive to Sudbury, and after she steps into the house that I hope will become my new home, she smiles. After some additional negotiating, the sellers and I sign an offer that night. I can't wait to tell the girls!

A few sleepless nights later, when I'm tossing and turning in bed, I wonder, *What am I doing?* Yes, my friends are going to lend me the down payment, but the reality is that Elizabeth is very ill, and we all are struggling. How am I going to have the time and strength to look after my girls the best I can, go back to work, and have enough income to pay all the bills? As the sun rises, my mood lifts when Olivia says, "Good morning, Mommy," as she gets ready for school, and Elizabeth greets me with a smile. They're happy about our new home. Now I know it's worth the risk. I know what's right to do.

Chapter 14

Hope and Fear

May 2001

It's the beginning of May, and we have hope that the experimental treatment will arrest the advancing cancer. We know the treatment will have a temporary, devastating impact, and it does. During the first week of the month, Elizabeth has seven stem-cell transfusions, one platelet transfusion, and two blood transfusions. By the end of the week, her blood cell counts return to normal. We're ecstatic to learn that Elizabeth's primary tumor, in her right femur, did not grow in the previous month. It's wonderful news!

To celebrate this good news and Mother's Day, Olivia and I prepare a picnic and buy chocolate treats and a glazed fruit tart at our favorite Concord bakery. We decide to picnic at a park in Lincoln, a site where the girls frequently played soccer. But first we stop to see Diana, who lives nearby and who lends me a chaise for Elizabeth. At the park, Olivia and I sit on a big blanket, and we spread out the picnic. My girls are chatting and talking about friends they want to see. I'm soaking in their banter, the warmth of the sun, and simply being with them. What a Mother's Day gift to have an oasis of happiness in the midst of difficulty.

However, our optimism about Elizabeth's condition is short-lived. By mid-May, Elizabeth's acute pain returns. We're not surprised that her right leg aches, but she's also in pain when she breathes. Last fall, they had told us that she had tumors in her lungs, but the initial chemotherapy treatments reduced their size and number. So, what's happening? Didn't they say the treatment was a success? Shouldn't the infusion have coated all of Elizabeth's tumors, stopped their growth, and given her a reprieve from suffering?

We have a terrible scare one morning when Elizabeth's central line is blocked. We rush to the ER because this could indicate a blood clot. We're afraid of the worst-case scenario, that she'd have to have emergency surgery to remove the central line and insert a new one. After hours of attempts to unblock the line at the ER, her doctor injects heparin into it, and this time the fluid immediately flows in. We look at each other in disbelief. How did that happen? The doctor asks Elizabeth, "Did anything unusual happen while you were in the ER?"

"Nothing, really, but I did have a few big sneezes."

"Well, you got rid of the kink with those big sneezes!" she says with a chuckle.

We leave the ER relieved but exhausted. My mind is spinning, and I can't stop wondering, *How long can I keep going back and forth and back and forth to the hospital and spending long days and sleepless nights there? And how many more tests can Elizabeth undergo, and how many more negative results can we hear?* I almost can't bear it anymore, yet I feel selfish for even thinking this. Elizabeth's suffering is the harshest. *But, my God, my God, I feel like* You've *abandoned me. Have* You *abandoned Elizabeth too? Where are* You? *Help us, help us. We need* You.

During the next week, I feel myself spiraling down and struggle to find ways to pull myself back up. Then out of the blue, Lisa calls and invites me to spend twenty-four hours with her in Newport. Susie agrees to look after Olivia and Elizabeth. Thankfully, there are no medical treatments planned for the next few days. I kiss my daughters good-bye and head off to my favorite city by the sea. When I get there, I fall into Lisa's arms, crying.

After a restorative lunch and nap, I walk along a beach. A brisk wind is blowing, and surfers in full bodysuits ride the waves. After a while, I sit on the beach next to a large boulder that protects me from the wind but gives me a full view of the ocean. The warmth of the sun on my face is comforting. I'm not sure how much time goes by, but I waken with a yawn. By the sparkling sea, I feel God's presence and peace.

Back at home, I'm clobbered by a new reality. The latest test results show more growth of Elizabeth's primary tumor. We're faced with another decision. The doctors recommend radiation to slow the growth of the tumor, but that has risks. Her femur is already weak, and radiation could cause a fracture, leading to cancerous cells invading her bloodstream. A fracture could lead to amputation. Despite the risks, Elizabeth wants the radiation to help relieve her pain. I can't bear this. Foreboding haunts my dreams.

Chapter 15
Unbearable
June 2001

One week until our move, and I have to pack up belongings at the condo where we lived with Neville. I've been dreading this day and have put it off as long as I could. To make it tolerable, my lawyer asks that Neville leave while I pack. Reluctantly, he agrees.

Nonetheless, to my dismay, when I walk into the kitchen, Neville is sitting at the computer with his back to me. He refuses to look at me or leave, and I don't have time to reschedule the packing. I hear a knock at the front door and let in Nandy, a dear, steadfast friend whom I first met when I moved to Lincoln. She's here to give me support and help me pack. When we step into the kitchen, I brace myself for Neville's angry accusations, but he sits in stony silence. I'm taut with fear.

I take a deep breath, ask Nandy to pack the kitchen, and head upstairs. At the top of the landing, I discover that Neville has kept the rooms closed up. I breathe in musty air and layers of dust that lie everywhere. I wonder why it feels creepy and realize I feel trapped. I shiver.

The girls' unmade beds and their wrinkled sheets look the same as when we hurriedly left eight months ago. As I pack Elizabeth's and Olivia's belongings, I try to hold back sobs, but they break through. I don't want to go into the master bedroom, but I have to. Windows are shut. Curtains drawn. I pack my belongings and label the boxes as fast as I can. When I get downstairs, I don't see Neville but know he's nearby. From the garage, the engine of his Jaguar roars.

A week later, a team of friends move our belongings. I feel an overwhelming sense of relief when I enter our new house. No more Neville. No more being controlled.

The following day, Elizabeth sits on her newly delivered queen bed in the living room while her uncle Peter finishes painting her bedroom. Beth drops by, and Elizabeth eagerly tells her, "Downstairs we'll have two sofas, a table, and a TV. Olivia's bedroom will be downstairs too, after a contractor does some work to make her room. Look at all the sunlight in the living room, and my bedroom is going to be just as I hoped it would!" Soon, we roll Elizabeth and her bed into her newly painted room. She's grinning while Beth unpacks and organizes her clothes.

When I bring Olivia home from school, she jumps out of the car and runs into the house. She shouts, "I'm here, Liz!" and runs down the hall to hug her sister. For the rest of the afternoon, Olivia, Elizabeth, and I banter back and forth as we decide how to arrange the furniture we've brought. Time passes quickly, and we're hungry and tired. I pick up take-out Chinese food, and we sit around a coffee table in the living room, eating and talking about the highlights of our day. We're here. We're safe. We're home.

Soon we have outdoor furniture, given to us by my sisters, and on warm afternoons, Elizabeth and I sit on the chaises in the sun and chat. She flips through fashion magazines. Olivia is keen to figure out what household items we need, so she makes a long list, and we go shopping. The girls have one more request. After years of their asking for a cat, I agree. At a shelter, Olivia sees a short-haired gray cat with black tiger stripes and white feet. She holds the cat, and it purrs. The vet tells us he is surprised because the cat has had a tough six weeks. Abandoned and sick, she's had many medical treatments and is wary of people. But as Olivia strokes the cat, she continues to purr. Olivia turns to me and says, "This is the cat, Mommy!"

Despite the vet's caution, when we get home with the cat, she promptly walks up the stairs and down the hall and then jumps onto Elizabeth's bed. It's amazing. She purrs as Elizabeth scratches between her ears. We name her Lilly.

Elizabeth is groaning in the night, and I check on her. She's asleep but twitching and moaning. I put my hand on her forehead and am relieved that she doesn't have a fever, but I wonder why she is in so much pain. Up to now we've clung to the hope that the experimental treatment would stop her tumors from multiplying. Now, a feeling of dread seeps into me. If that treatment doesn't save her, what will? Could radiation?

Despite the risks explained a few weeks ago, Elizabeth does begin radiation treatments on her primary tumor in her right femur. After three weeks of treatments, this area continues to swell. The contrast in the size of her left and right legs, especially at the knee, is alarming. Concerned after seeing an X-ray, Dr. Kin asks us to see him in the children's clinic.

Elizabeth starts talking first. "Why is my knee getting bigger and bigger, and why does it hurt so much?"

"Well, it could be in response to the experimental treatment, and it's flaring up," Dr. Kin says. Then he hesitates. "Or it could be that the tumor is not responding and is growing."

After a pause Elizabeth asks, "I know that you are trying to find out about other experimental treatments. Have you found any?"

"I've tried and will keep trying. My colleagues and I have been searching through research papers and databases." He looks at me and then Elizabeth. "But we haven't found one yet. I'd like my nurse to schedule a full-body CT scan. We'll confirm a time as soon as we can."

We meet with Dr. Kin again to get the results. His expression is grave. "I know you've always asked me to tell you the truth, Elizabeth, so I will. I have very tough news." Gently he continues, "Your imaging shows that your primary tumor has grown, and you also have tumors in your lungs, ribs, sternum, hips, neck, and skull."

She gasps. Tears stream down her face. After a few minutes, she asks in a hushed voice, "What else can you do, Dr. Kin?"

"I'll keep searching for new treatments."

"What will happen next? I mean if I don't have more treatments?"

"Your tumors will multiply, and you will be in more pain. I will prescribe a morphine patch that will adhere to your arm and relieve your pain. You'll wear the patch twenty-four hours a day and change it for a new one every three days."

"And what else will happen?"

"You'll have a harder time breathing."

She whispers, "Why?"

"Air passes through healthy lungs easily. But you have many small tumors blocking your lungs, and this slows down the passage of air. As your disease worsens, it will—"

She finishes the sentence. "Get harder to breathe."

He nods. "We will set you up with a tank that will pump oxygen into your nose. This will help you breathe better."

"And then?"

He hesitates, takes a deep breath, and continues, "The passages in your lungs will be blocked by tumors and will fill up with water. It will be harder and harder to breathe."

"I'll stop breathing?"

He nods. In silence, she slumps forward in her chair.

On our drive home, Elizabeth watches people riding bikes, jogging, and pushing strollers along the Esplanade. She turns to me and says, "Mommy, I'll never be a bride."

Chapter 16

Last Wishes

Late June to Mid-July 2001

As the early light of dawn seeps into my room, I am swamped with grief. In only a few minutes, I realize that I can't allow my anguish to haunt the remaining months of Elizabeth's life. I have to take action and gather every resource I can to bring as much comfort and joy as possible into all of our lives.

The following morning, I call the Make-A-Wish Foundation and explain the situation. I ask if it's at all possible to organize a trip within four to six weeks. To my great relief, she calls me the following morning and says, "Yes, it is."

Elizabeth perks up at this wonderful news. "Oh, Mommy! I want to go to an island, stay in a hotel next to a beach, and tan in the sun and swim." We look at options, and she decides on Bermuda because it offers everything she wants and is only a two-hour flight away.

Elizabeth asks, "Can we bring Annie and Molly on my Make-A-Wish trip too?"

"That's a wonderful idea, but I'm not sure if friends can be included. I'll call right away and ask."

I call the volunteer, ask if we could go to Bermuda, and ask if Annie and Molly could come too. I explain to her that Annie has visited Elizabeth almost every week since her diagnosis, and how supportive Annie and her mother, Molly, have been of both my girls. She responds, "We can definitely arrange for a trip to Bermuda, but I'll need to check to find out if we can include Annie and Molly. I'll call you back tomorrow."

The following morning the Make-A-Wish Foundation calls back and says, "Yes! Your family can stay in a beautiful seaside hotel for six days. Annie and Molly can go too! In a few days, I'll call back with all of the details." Quickly, the Make-A-Wish trip is scheduled for July 6–12.

Even before this adventure, a new milestone for Elizabeth approaches. July 1 is Elizabeth's fourteenth birthday. Olivia and I consider possibilities to make her birthday special. But before we have made a plan, my friend Lisa calls and asks Elizabeth, "Would you like to celebrate your fourteenth birthday in a penthouse suite at the Newport Marriott? You can bring friends and one of your friends' mothers. It has rooms looking out onto the harbor."

"Wow! That would be fun, Lisa!"

A few days later, my girls and their friends arrive at the suite while I stay home to gather my strength. They have an expansive view onto Newport Harbor filled with yachts from all over the world. Two-story elegant motorboats, a ten-story cruise ship, and small sailboats crisscross the harbor. Elizabeth's friends swim in the indoor pool and soak in the sauna. That night, Lisa brings Elizabeth and her friends lobster, their favorite meal, along with corn on the cob and a chocolate birthday cake. While propped up in bed, Elizabeth beams happily in the company of her sister and best friends. They talk late into the night and sleep in in the morning, as they have done so many times on so many overnights before.

The next day, after a bountiful brunch, Elizabeth and her friends say good-bye to Lisa.

"Thank you, thank you, Lisa! You made my birthday so special. I had the best time!"

Her friends echo, "We did too! Thank you!"

Two hours later, Elizabeth crawls into bed at home, exhausted but happy, still in the glow of her birthday retreat.

Days later, we pack for our upcoming trip to Bermuda. Elizabeth is excited, but I'm worried. Compared to two weeks ago, she is noticeably weaker and thinner. She asks, "Mommy, I really want to go, but how long will it take to get there? I'm so tired."

"It will take about forty-five minutes to drive to Logan, and we'll need to be at the airport at least one hour before the plane leaves. The flight to Bermuda takes less than two hours. After we arrive, we have to go through customs, and then we'll have a short ride to the hotel. If everything goes well, door-to-door it will take five hours, or perhaps six if we have some delays."

"That sounds long but okay. I'd like to have a wheelchair in the airports."

I have not told the girls about one part of the Make-A-Wish plan. On July 6, a black limousine pulls into the driveway. I call to the girls, "It's time to go. Look out the window!"

Olivia shouts, "I can't believe it, Mommy! We're going to the airport in a limousine?"

"We'll be like movie stars! Yahoo!" Elizabeth hollers.

Annie and Molly arrive, and we all pile into the limousine.

Despite the comfortable ride to the airport, and a smooth flight, Elizabeth is exhausted when we get off the plane. A Bermudian is waiting for us with a wheelchair, and Elizabeth weakly climbs in. The rest of us gather our bags. I'm worried that it could take us another hour to get through the customs line, and Elizabeth can barely hold herself up in her wheelchair. Just then, a customs agent stands up and walks toward us. I say with a smile, "We're here for the Make-A-Wish trip."

He replies, "Yes, I'm expecting you. Let's see how I can help."

He motions us to carry our bags over to him, and then he slides each one of them to the other side of the customs gate. Then he glances at each passport and says, "Have a wonderful time on our island! A driver is waiting for you in the pickup area outside."

The next morning, I'm standing in clear turquoise waters next to Elizabeth, who rests on a float in a protected lagoon. The gentle rising and falling waves cradle her like the rising and falling notes of a lullaby. Ten months have gone by since Elizabeth's diagnosis. Here she is, relieved to be free of weekly rounds of treatments, of nausea and pain, of days and nights where she's barely had the strength to crawl into bed. She looks peaceful, at rest in this tropical paradise.

After an hour in the sun, I pull her float to shore. Elizabeth slides off into waist-high water and leans on my shoulder as we slowly walk toward the beach. Her wheelchair waits on the paved path nearby. With my support, Elizabeth slowly lowers herself into the wheelchair, and I push her back toward the hotel.

She turns to me and says, "Mommy, aren't you glad that you have two daughters?"

"Yes, you know I've always been so happy to have daughters."

"Well, at least you'll have one."

I step in front of her, bend down, and say, "Honey, I'll always have two because you'll be with me always."

During the next few days, Elizabeth sleeps more and more. Some afternoons, I lie on her bed and she holds my hand. I read to her, and before long she falls asleep. In the early evenings, we help her stand up, and with one arm draped around Olivia and one around Annie, they walk onto the patio. Elizabeth rests on a chaise lounge and looks out to the ocean, watching the cresting and falling waves. We eat fresh fish, local vegetables, and fruit, and we talk about the day's activities. As the sun sets, the cicadas sing their nightly song. She nods off to sleep.

Some evenings, Olivia lies next to Elizabeth and reads while her sister dozes. Olivia, too, has mellowed in this serene setting. Her edginess, so apparent over the last few months, has vanished. She is gentle, attentive, and patient. Each of those evenings, I look from my bed to where they are lying and am overwhelmed with longing for the years when cancer was not part of our lives, when they tussled and tumbled together like two bear cubs, and when they used to run into my arms for hugs.

One evening, after Elizabeth has fallen asleep and Olivia and Annie are watching TV, Molly and I walk down to the beach. We sit on chairs under a thatched-roof cabana. Moonlight shimmers on the darkened waters; constellations twinkle above. The silence is broken by my muffled sobs.

Molly leans forward and says, "This is a great gift. Liz is next to the sea, her favorite place to be. She's with Olivia and Annie, who love her so much. She knows how much you love her, Faith. Olivia knows your love too."

Molly rubs my back and sits close to me until my sobbing ebbs. "You're an amazing mom to both Olivia and Liz. You're strong, Faith. You have faced enormous challenges head-on. You'll find the strength you'll need for Liz and Olivia in the months ahead. I know you will."

I lean toward Molly and rest my head on her shoulder. Thousands of stars glisten above us. Moonlight bathes the sea.

Chapter 17

One Last Gift

Mid to Late July 2001

Olivia drops the suitcases in the front hall while I support Elizabeth as we walk into our house. Leaving our tropical paradise and its peaceful surroundings is tough. We're back to our harsh reality.

In a few minutes, however, I hear Olivia's upbeat voice from the lower level. "Come down here, Mommy and Liz!"

Elizabeth cries, "Oh, the family room is ready! The yellow walls look so good, and the big, comfy sofa has arrived. I'm so excited to have our own TV!"

"Come see my bedroom," Olivia says. "It's peach, my favorite color, and look at how well the curtains go with it!"

Both chime, "Thank you, Mommy!"

That night, I hear them chatting, calling friends, and surfing channels on the TV. I nod off to sleep happily.

In the morning, sunlight bathes our cozy kitchen. I look out the window onto the wood deck and the semicircular gravel patio edged by variegated ivy. Beyond lies a verdant lawn, centuries-old stone walls, and a sparsely wooded glen. I breathe in peace.

My sense of well-being is short-lived. These days Elizabeth is too weak to raise her head off her pillow. Like an advancing enemy, tumor after tumor invades her lungs, hips, sternum, ribs, and even her skull. A startlingly large tumor bulges on the side of her neck.

I lean against her bedroom wall and watch the labored rise and fall of her chest as she sleeps. *Why, God, why didn't you inflict me? Why, God, why not me?* I am breaking up inside and don't think I can ever be put back together. No one, no one can save me from shattering.

Profound sadness also cloaks Olivia. She seems slowed down by sorrow. She's losing her dearest friend, her little sister. Elizabeth is slowly drifting away from us, and we know we are powerless to draw her back. Our trinity, our beloved trinity is breaking up before our eyes.

In the waning weeks of July, waves of kindness break to the surface. Friends, especially Annie, visit Elizabeth frequently, and my sisters and friends keep in constant touch to lift our spirits. One day, the manager of a country club on Cape Cod, where my parents are members, invites us to stay for a weekend by the sea. We accept immediately, and I ask my cousin Julia to join us.

Since I was a child, this nineteenth-century weathered-shingle manse has been a favorite place for my family and cousins to gather together. Memories flood back of playing on the beach, swimming with my sisters, frolicking with Julia's family, and battling on the tennis courts.

Here we are again, settled into a two-bedroom suite, in very different times. Julia and I are determined to make it special. In the evening, trays brimming with seafood are brought to our rooms because Elizabeth's too weak to get to the dining room. In the morning, a server brings us fresh orange juice, scrambled eggs, and buttery croissants. After a morning nap, Elizabeth props herself up in bed and looks out onto the sea. Julia, Olivia, and I keep her company.

Feeling stronger in the afternoon, Elizabeth asks to go to the beach. She sits on the edge of her bed, wraps one arm around my shoulder and one around Olivia's, and hobbles down the hall to the waiting elevator. After we reach the ground floor, we support her as she slowly navigates a twenty-foot grassy path to a flight of stairs to the beach. Elizabeth slowly reaches the sand. Exhausted, she collapses onto a chaise. Olivia puts a pillow behind her sister's head, and Elizabeth dozes off to sleep. We sit silently nearby, listening to calls of the seabirds and children playing in the sand. That night in our room, we dine on lobster and corn on the cob. Later, the sounds of waves gently breaking on the beach cradle us to sleep.

On Sunday morning, my muffled sobs waken Julia. She sits on the edge of my bed and holds my hand until my crying ebbs. After a while, we go to the girls' room. Olivia looks at her sleeping sister, haunted by what's happening.

Chapter 18
Final Breaths
August 2001

It's three weeks later, and Elizabeth's breathing is strenuous as she sleeps, despite the assistance of an oxygen machine. Low moans come from her lips. She rolls over and wakens, and slowly her day begins. She labors to sit up on the edge of the bed, waiting for dizziness to subside. Her ribs are visible through her thin cotton top. She hobbles to the shower and rinses briefly, brushes her teeth, hobbles more, and leans on the doorjamb to catch her breath. After a few more steps, she collapses into bed. Each breath is a struggle. She replaces the oxygen tubes in her nose and breathes in. She dozes off for a while, and when she stirs, she looks at me.

"Mommy, I don't mind that I'm leaving now. That may be very hard for you to hear, but I've tried so hard for one year. I'm not scared—it feels like I'm going on a trip. I just don't know where I'm going."

Heaving sobs come from my body.

"Mommy, you'll need to keep busy and be with your friends. I want you to remarry and be happy again."

Later that morning, she feels a bit stronger and looks at fashion catalogs. I'm elated when she wants to place an order for a shirt she likes. Elizabeth calls and tells the store's rep the item number, size, and color that she wants. After waiting a moment, she turns to me and says, "It's on back order until October."

She speaks into the phone. "Well, that's too late. Thank you anyway."

This is more than I can bear.

Only a few of Elizabeth's friends visit now. It's summer, and many are away at camp or with their families on vacation. The reality is they can't stand to see their friend suffering. The few close friends who visit Elizabeth handle her illness the best they can. When she has the strength, she props herself up in her bed and chats with them. Sometimes, they just sit quietly on her bed or beside it.

At the beginning of the month, Molly calls to find out how Elizabeth is. When I say her condition is rapidly worsening, Molly immediately asks if Annie can visit right away. For the next three Mondays, Annie and her father fly from Halifax, where they are vacationing, so Annie can visit. Elizabeth is thrilled. On each visit, I hear them chatting and even laughing. My heart lightens until a jagged pain seizes me, aching for both of them.

Olivia and I are by Elizabeth's bedside day and night. My sisters, parents, and closest friends visit a few times a week. Life goes on around us. Some days, I hear the bang of the basketball as my neighbor's son tosses it at the backboard, see children on bikes, and watch people jog by. But I'm no longer living in that world. I'm on a barren shore watching my youngest child drift away from me.

One evening, Elizabeth whispers to me, "I'm ready for hospice care, Mommy."

Numb, I make the call the next day. Soon nurses and social workers arrive. Not only do they care for Elizabeth, but the social workers also take time with Olivia too. Calmly and quietly they come and go. They gently prepare me for what will happen next. I shift from being calm to wanting to scream. But I can't. Not now.

That night outside my window, the cicadas sing their nightly song, but their buzzing is no longer soothing as it was when I was young. *How is it, God, that the summer days and nights are carefree for so many, yet we are living in a nightmare?*

Elizabeth struggles to breathe and slips in and out of consciousness. The hospice nurses increase Elizabeth's pain medications and oxygen supply. One night toward the end, Olivia is sleeping beside Elizabeth. I wake at six thirty and check on them. Olivia looks at me anxiously. Elizabeth's struggle to breathe has worsened. I call the hospice nurses, my parents, and my sisters.

My father and sisters sit at the foot of Elizabeth's bed. Olivia and I lie on either side of her. With great effort she says, "Cuddle me." We hold her and tell her how much we love her and how brave she has been. The nurses raise Elizabeth's head gently to give larger doses of liquid morphine. Outside on our patio, my mother and niece pray.

As five o'clock approaches, Elizabeth is taking fewer breaths. I know the end is near. Olivia is asleep next to her. I waken her to tell her that we are losing Elizabeth. We both hold her and speak words of love softly. Moments later, she is still. Elizabeth is gone.

I cradle her in my arms. Her face is serene, her eyes closed, her body warm against mine. I'm barely breathing. Piercing cries stab me. Olivia is howling a keening cry, as though she had been slashed with a sword. Minutes go by, or maybe hours—I do not know. I feel soft kisses on my cheeks. Hazy figures move around the room. Olivia kisses her sister one last time.

Distant murmurings become more audible now. The nurses tell me they have ordered a hearse, and it will be here soon. "It's best, Faith and Olivia, for you to leave the room before the stretcher arrives."

I hold Elizabeth, and then with all the strength I can gather, I gently let go. Olivia and I walk out of the room. Olivia goes outside to be with my mother, and I lie on my bed behind a closed door. I hear the front door open and wheels rolling down the hallway. They're here. I close my eyes and pray. Ten minutes later, the house is silent. I go outside. My mother is holding Olivia on her lap. My father and sisters reach out to hug me.

Chapter 19

Sorrow

September 8, 2001

On September 8, as Olivia and I approach the church where Elizabeth's service will be held, we're overwhelmed by the hundreds of people gathered to wish Elizabeth good-bye. Some reach out to hold our hands or give us a kiss. Others hang back, perhaps uneasy witnessing our suffering. Moments before we enter the church, I grasp Olivia's hand.

Elizabeth had told us that she wanted Olivia and me to wear beautiful dresses, not gloomy ones, at her funeral. Mine's batik with a sweep of lavender and rose-colored flowers. Olivia's has pink and red roses on a black background.

A sea of kind faces turns to greet us. I am awed by the vast number of friends and acquaintances who came out of love for all of us: Julia and her husband David, sitting with their thirteen-year-old daughter and ten-year-old sons; Beth, Diana, Lisa, Nandy, and their families; friends from Smith College whom I haven't seen in years; childhood friends; work colleagues; and Elizabeth's oncologists. Tears spring to my eyes. Olivia nods to her classmates and soccer and swim team friends. The sanctuary is filled with Elizabeth's favorite summer flowers in lavender, cornflower blue, and pale pink hues. Rays of sunlight pour into the sanctuary. We sit down in the left-front pew with my sisters and parents by our side.

To my surprise, my sister Sarah has arranged for a renowned choir and organist to provide the music for Elizabeth's service. The sounds of the organ and choir set the peaceful but sorrowful tone.

When Elizabeth knew she would not survive much longer, she asked two ministers, who were attentive throughout her illness, to give her eulogies. In their own way, each speaks of Elizabeth's compassion, her strength in adversity, her humor, and the impact she had on those around her. One minister reads a poem I wrote, and the other reads a letter that Olivia wrote to her sister. A few minutes later, we sing "Sleep My Child, Sleep." I can't hold back my sobs. Olivia leans into me, and we hold each other.

Elizabeth's fourteen-year-old friend Annie speaks from the altar about her love and admiration for her best friend. Annie is remarkably composed and articulate, displaying the characteristics that Elizabeth loved her for. I can't help but think how proud Elizabeth would have been.

Toward the end of the service, the choir sings "Pie Jesu." The voices and organ music blend in a mystical harmony. The highest notes, so clearly voiced, lift to the peaks of the sanctuary, transporting us closer to where Elizabeth's spirit now lives. An awed silence follows. Even though we had hoped that Elizabeth's funeral would provide some comfort and closure, now that it's over, we're devastated. She's truly, utterly gone.

Part 2
"Night Sky"

Grief is dusk, the familiar still visible in the fading light.
Despair is midnight, dark and heavy with clouds.
Hope is a bright star sparkling on a moonless night.

Chapter 20

Terror

September 11, 2001

Three days after the funeral, Olivia calls me in a panic. "Mommy, have you heard? Planes flew into the World Trade Towers, and they've collapsed! Come and get me. Everybody's going home."

I'm confused. I haven't had the radio or TV on this morning, and I know nothing about the events. As I drive to the high school, I hear the news on the radio. Olivia gets into the car and says, "I'm scared. I can't believe this. The teacher told us that thousands of people may have died. What else is going to happen?"

"I don't know. We'll find out when we're home."

When we get there, we watch the news and see the horrifying images of the Trade Towers falling. At the same time, we hear a helicopter flying over our neighborhood. Olivia asks, "Do you think they'll drop bombs, Mommy?"

I turn the TV off. "No, honey, this is happening in New York, not here." I don't know anything else to say.

I don't turn on the TV for the rest of the day to protect Olivia and me. We're already living in our own nightmare of Elizabeth's death. The suffering of so many strangers is too much for us to take in.

In the early afternoon, Julia's older sister calls me, her voice pitched high and anxious. "We haven't been able to reach Julia and

David to see if they're okay. Their phone is always busy. You know that David works in the Trade Towers, don't you?"

I feel like I've been punched in the stomach. I knew that David worked in New York City, but despite all the years I've been close to Julia, I did not know he worked in the Trade Towers. Suddenly, this horror becomes real to me.

"Please, will you try to get through to Julia?" her sister pleads. "Call me if you do, and I'll do the same."

A few minutes later I call Julia, and a stranger's voice answers, "The Rathkey residence." I identify myself and ask to speak to Julia. After a pause, she says, "She's upstairs with her children. She'll call you when she can."

My stomach sinks. Something must be wrong.

I don't hear from Julia for two days, but I do learn that David did not come home on the night of September 11. When Julia calls, she blurts between sobs, "We still don't know where David is. The children think he's lying in a hospital or walking around with amnesia. But I'm certain he was killed. At night, I feel his presence beside me. I feel—no, I know—that he doesn't want to leave us."

My heart aches for Julia and her children. I can almost see the floodwaters of grief surging toward her with such force that she won't be able to escape. I know. After Elizabeth's death, I'm drowning in grief.

As hard as it is to attend David's funeral so soon after Elizabeth's, I must be there to support Julia and her children. So, three weeks later, Olivia and I drive to northern New Jersey and sit in a church overflowing with people. Julia's children are tucked by her side. Friends remember David's quiet strength, his love of Julia and his children, and his dedication to coaching soccer teams. In fact, dozens of children whom he coached are present.

Despite my intent to stay strong during the service, when the music begins, my eyes fill with tears. Parents wrap their arms around their children and quietly cry. Not only is innocence shattered for the young, but parents are stunned by the sudden insecurity of terrorism on our shores.

Chapter 21

Anger and Despair

Fall 2001 – Spring 2002

During the day, I feel like I'm scrambling up a steep mountain trail and gasping for breath. My pulse quickens, my chest contracts, my legs cramp. At night, I fall asleep exhausted, even if I have only raked leaves, sobbed, and rested. Life overwhelms me. Chores that I used to sail through before, like shopping, are rugged. Sometimes in a grocery store, I see people I know. I slip down a different aisle to avoid them; other times I stop and we hug. One day, I walk by the Little Bite brownies that Elizabeth loved. I run out of the store crying, jarred to my core.

Each morning I drive Olivia to high school and ask about her upcoming day. Silence is her usual response. Many afternoons, she calls me from school and says she's going to a friend's house. When she's home in the evenings, she either closes herself in her bedroom or watches TV. But the effort of holding in her grief overcomes her when she's in the shower. I hear her sobbing behind the locked door. I feel powerless to help her, and I wonder why she hides her grief from me.

One day in the late fall, Olivia's steely reserve fractures, and she erupts with caustic words. She's angry that I was MIA during the last year. Angry that I didn't leave her father years ago. Angry that

Elizabeth suffered and fought for her life, but death grabbed her in the end. She tells me that she'll never believe in God again.

As the winter months slowly pass, I spend most of my days indoors. I read books about loss and grieving. I read books about healing. I read books about coping. I pray for guidance. It dawns on me that my isolation makes me a captive of despair. I take a few tentative steps outside my front door. I accept invitations to have meals with friends and take walks in the woods, and I gaze at the stars in the night sky. I slowly discover that when I have companionship, I feel a whisper of relief. Alone, I can't stop sobbing.

I begin a new practice of writing before I fall asleep at night. This gives me a way to remember joyful and painful times, moments of strength and periods of collapse, hilltops of hope and caverns of despair. Over time, I learn how to express my feelings rather than keeping them locked inside.

On her sixteenth birthday, Olivia and I celebrate quietly at home because she doesn't want a party. I make a fire, and we eat dinner. Two of her friends drop by unexpectedly, and Olivia perks up. We settle in around the fireplace, talk about Elizabeth, and laugh when we remember her escapades. Soon our laughter gives way to tears. Olivia sobs, "I want to stop crying every day."

Her friend responds, "Elizabeth deserves our tears."

Gradually the hours of daylight increase, and buds of pink, coral, and yellow burst forth on the trees and shrubberies. One sunny morning, Olivia walks into my bedroom and asks, "Mommy, are you awake?" She crawls into my bed, and I hug her. Lilly jumps up and makes herself comfortable on Olivia's chest, and she scratches our cat on her forehead.

Olivia whispers, "We are a new family."

"Yes, we are."

As the weather warms, I soak in moments of happiness when gardening with Olivia or having tea with a friend on the sunny patio. I discover moments of peace in the blossoming of spring.

Chapter 22

Grieving and Healing
Spring 2002 – Summer 2002

Moments of hope in the spring give me an unexpected boost of energy, and I consider returning to work. I'm surprised at this change. After Elizabeth's death, it was as though the complex ways that the mind works had been short-circuited, and I barely functioned. Now, as the days lengthen, I'm able to concentrate for periods of time and follow a daily routine. The unbearable weight that I've been carrying night and day has lessened. Over time, I discover the cost of this shift.

I channel my new energy to find a job so that I can afford my mortgage, have health insurance, and support my daughter. I consider the pros and cons of working in Boston and soon build up my courage to call the manager I worked for twelve years ago. I tell her of my interest in returning to her department, and to my total surprise, she immediately replies, "I'll call you back in a few days. I want you to return." Four days later, I'm welcomed by my former colleagues.

During this same time, a friend I haven't seen in years visits me. I make some tea, and we sit down on my living room sofa. With tears in her eyes she says, "I was so sorry to learn about Elizabeth's death. I can't begin to imagine all that you have been through."

She reaches out, and we hug.

She continues, "How are you and Olivia doing?"

"Some days, I can manage to get through the day. Some days, I can't stop sobbing. Olivia is a sophomore in high school. The daily routine is stabilizing for her, but she's devastated."

She says, "I have a particular reason for visiting you today. Eight of our college friends got together and thought about how we could help."

She reaches into her bag, brings out a check, and gives it to me. Tears well up in my eyes. Once again, I'm bowled over by the generous acts of the growing community supporting me. When I fall asleep that night, I whisper, "All will be well."

In the coming weeks, I dive into work, first getting up to speed with recent changes in the international employee benefits industry and learning my role on the sales and service team. Before long, I'm writing proposals for multinational clients, training new staff, and assisting my account executive. Besides the financial security, I find unexpected benefits at work. I enjoy having a daily routine, engaging with colleagues, and during my lunch break, taking walks along the streets of Back Bay and in the Boston Common. I watch mothers and children feeding ducks, families riding on the swan boats, and others picnicking outdoors. I begin to feel part of the rhythm of life.

But as the weeks turn into months, my new commitment takes an unexpected toll. Commuting three hours each day, eight-hour days at my desk, and growing neck and back pain are exhausting to me. Olivia is reacting to these changes too. After her initial happiness about my job, she becomes angry that I'm away for eleven hours every day. After school, she either visits friends or has to come home to an empty house. She both misses me and is mad at me. I'm shattered that an unanticipated rift is growing between us, and I don't know what to do about it.

One morning while working in my cubical, guttural sobs escape from me. My manager motions me to come into her office and asks if there is anything she can do. I shake my head, sobbing. She looks at me with concern and suggests that I leave for the day.

On the train ride home, I call my therapist, David, and he encourages me to visit him that afternoon. I'm torn between wanting to drive home, crawl under my covers, and cry, or take him up on his offer. I decide to see him.

David asks, "What happened today?"

"I'm exhausted by my long days. I'm upset because even though I have a good job, I can't quite make ends meet. I'm worried because Olivia is pulling away from me. And I can't sleep."

Then I burst out, "And I'm so sad and scared about the first anniversary of Elizabeth's death. It's only a month away. I can't bear that she's been gone for a whole year. I can't cope. . . ."

David sits quietly until I calm down. He hands me a copy of the Buddhist prayer of lovingkindness. He has given this before and knows it calms me.

May I be filled with lovingkindness. May I be well.

May I be peaceful and at ease. May I be happy.

After my breathing steadies, he shifts forward in his chair, his kind blue eyes focusing on me. "You've undertaken a lot in the last four months. It makes complete sense that you're exhausted. Can you take a week of vacation? Being home and resting and planning some activities to do together with Olivia will help both of you."

I nod.

David continues, "And I have another idea too. Rather than anticipate with fear the first anniversary of Elizabeth's death, why don't you plan something special to mark this date and honor Elizabeth? If you craft a plan, then you can have some control over what will happen on that day, rather than be afraid about what that day might do to you."

On the drive home, I feel better . . . wiped out, but better. I crawl under the covers for the rest of the day.

That weekend I call Lisa and tell her about my recent meeting with David. She asks, "Do you have any ideas about what you want to do on Elizabeth's anniversary day?"

"All I know is that I want to be home with Olivia and a few friends, and in my garden."

"You've been wanting to improve the look of your front garden." Lisa says, "Would you like to plant a garden in memory of Elizabeth? If you do, I'd like to help you. Let's talk about what you'd like to plant."

After discussing ideas, we decide on myrtle for ground cover, box-woods for height, pink peonies and white roses for color. "All you need to do is to find some strong men to pull out the old yews and to dig holes for the new plants. I'll bring the supplies and the plants and be at your house in the morning."

On the anniversary of Elizabeth's death, we start work. Lisa arrives, her van overflowing. Olivia, my sister Sarah, and two men friends are ready to help. We pull out the overgrown yews and errant roots and till the now-barren garden bed with picks, shovels, and trowels to remove rocks and roots. We shovel in compost and rake the garden bed smooth. The men dig, and one by one we settle in each plant. From time to time, we pause to drink lemonade or iced tea.

Rather than feeling exhausted and overwhelmed by grief, I feel deep peace. Working in the earth and transforming an overgrown garden into one that reflects beauty unexpectedly creates a new sense of harmony and strengthens my connection to Olivia, Lisa, and Sarah. Elizabeth has given us a gift on this day. One of comfort, hope, and serenity.

Chapter 23

Finding Comfort

Fall 2002 – Summer 2004

How do I begin a new life without a partner, without Elizabeth, and with a maturing Olivia who needs me less? Once I was the center of our family's orbit; now there is no gravity to keep my planets close. I've been pulled far away into a new galaxy. I have to find my bearings to survive.

It's daunting. It's scary. It's dark.

And yet, within me there still lies a spark, one that lights up intermittently. David works with me to grow that spark so I can begin to find a way out of the darkness that envelops me. He encourages me to continue to write, and each night, before I turn out my light, I scrawl out the raging fear trapped inside, wrestling with it like a wounded lioness would fight pursuing hunters.

And to calm the turbulence I'm experiencing, David encourages me to go on a seven-day silent retreat at a nearby monastery. I enter this hermitage torn apart by pain and grief. During the week, I walk long hours along a sprawling tidal river and paths in the woods, and across newly hayed fields. The longer I walk, the better I breathe, the calmer I feel, and the clearer I think. The quiet, gentle presence of the brothers, the nourishing meals, and the hours of prayers fill me with peace. I welcome its return like a mother would embrace a lost child who stumbled back home.

While I'm on retreat, I write this poem.

Where Do I Go from Here?

Where will I begin?
My life is so changed from what it has been.

Where do I start?

Will I sit by a pond in the cool sunlight?
Will I walk in the woods, which are anticipating spring?

Will I hold my grieving daughter?
Will I have lunch with friends and hear news of their
*   families?*
Will I fold up my dark winter clothes,
and fill my drawers with the lighter clothes of spring?

Perhaps I'll walk in an open, rough field,
lined by stone walls, tall pine trees and filled with
*   whispering winds;*
where the light is bright and shadows are few;
a field large enough for all my memories to flow through,
and where there is room for me to move.

I will go into this field,
and step into something new;
each step remembering,
each step reconciling,
each step guiding me toward a place I am longing to be.

Over the following years, my parents, sisters, and close friends and their families invite me to seaside resorts and mountain lakes they frequent. We walk along beaches and search for shells. We swim in tidal currents that sweep us along the shoreline. We picnic on docks and cook fresh seafood at night. They all include me as if I am one of their family. Family life now has a new definition for me.

Increasingly, in her last year in high school, Olivia spends more time with friends than she does at home. I often feel a jolt as I step into a dark, empty house. I long to see pairs of sneakers scattered in the front hall, hear the girls shout, "Is it dinnertime yet?" and ask them, "How was your day?" But the only response I hear is the creak of the floorboards as I walk up the stairs. Another reality to adjust to.

Even while I know it's normal for older teenagers to prefer to spend more time with friends than family, it's hard for me. Some days I ache, longing to have her home more, and wishing that Elizabeth was with us. She would have been in high school now too. Instead, many nights I set the table for one.

When I fall asleep, I frequently think of the last year of Elizabeth's life. I remember when a friend, whom I had known since I was nineteen years old, began visiting Elizabeth when we were living at my sister's house. Henry brought her gifts of macaroons, maple syrup, and pancake mix, but mainly he brought good cheer. Even though he spent most of the time with Elizabeth, his caring lifted my spirits too. The day after Elizabeth's death, Henry visited me. I was strengthened by his willingness to be with me when I was at my most raw and vulnerable, especially in the face of many others' fear of my grief.

Years later, Henry calls me. It's comforting to talk with him because he's almost like family, and in time I see how much he cares about Olivia and me. As Henry and I spend time together, I begin to shed the protective layers wrapped tightly around me, like a creature that molts its outer skin to expose the more vulnerable one beneath. He listens with care when I share traumas of my past, and he offers support as I struggle with my ever-changing relationship with Olivia. His ways are steadfast and dependable, and when he wraps me in his bear hug, my loneliness melts away.

Chapter 24
Facing My Past
Fall 2004

In hindsight, when I look back on the first three years after Elizabeth's death, I realize that my thought process had lost its acuity. Prior to being in a state of grieving, I had a sharp recollection for details, but while being shrouded in sorrow, I couldn't remember birthdays of family and friends, much of what I did at work, or who had called an hour before. One day when I was driving Olivia to an appointment, she said that I drove through three red lights. I have no recollection of that at all.

Olivia fared only slightly better than I did. She came down with mono and missed many days of school. Even when she recovered, she lacked the energy that she'd once had. She didn't want to take ballet lessons anymore or join a club soccer team. She could still focus on her academic work, and she excelled in school. In the late fall of her senior year, she began to get excited about going to college. With her strong grades, she was accepted to many. After visiting her first choice in the spring, she enthusiastically accepted her admission to a college in Charleston.

Slowly, my mind shed layers of blurriness, and I could think more clearly. The timing was far from ideal, however, because I was bracing for another loss when Olivia would soon leave home and begin a new life at college.

It's late August, near the third anniversary of Elizabeth's death, as I look out the window on my return flight from South Carolina to Massachusetts. My chest tightens and my heartbeat races. I want the plane to reverse direction and fly south. Back to where I've left Olivia, who is beginning her freshman year. I'm happy for her that she's excited to begin college, but it's hitting me hard. I want to see her daily life and know she's safe at night.

As I choke up, I want to return to a time when I was a mother to a younger Olivia who ran into the kitchen after being dropped off by the school bus, bursting with news and ready for a homemade snack. I want to see her confidently singing the lead in the middle school musical and chasing the soccer ball down the field on weekends. I want to play cards with her at night.

In my reverie, I remember eighteen years ago, when I looked into her infant-blue eyes and felt a stronger connection to life and love than I had ever experienced before. God gave me the greatest gift one can receive, a child to love and to nurture. I'm not ready for this separation.

I drift in my daydream to the time when I first met Olivia's father, two months after I graduated from college and moved to Boston. He was a worldly photographer of fine art who brought new perspectives to my worldviews. Soon, he was treating me like I was his one and only true love. I fell under his spell.

At this same time, I started a promising new career in international employee benefits. I found it exciting to work with people from around the world. I had a heady feeling of freedom and enthusiastically jumped into a far-flung world quite different from that of my youth.

Over the next two years, I traveled with Neville to Paris, where his mother and stepfather, who was an exiled Russian aristocrat, lived. I dined with royal families who had been uprooted when European countries fell to communist dictators. I was dazzled by stories of their glamorous pre-communist lives, the masterpieces of art in their Parisian apartments, and the warmth with which they welcomed me. We went to a wedding of a young Hapsburg in Brussels, and we danced among the young royals of many European countries. I was head over heels in love when Neville proposed to me. We were married in 1984.

My career was advancing well. We settled into a renovated carriage house in Charlestown and were making new friends. To my great joy, I reconnected with Lisa, who was living on Beacon Hill.

But while I recounted the exciting times with family and friends, over time I became afraid to share the tough times with them. Occasionally at first, and then more frequently, Neville's deep-seated rage began to show itself. When he disagreed with his mother, or even his clients who offered a different viewpoint, they suddenly felt the icy chill of his cold rage. His inappropriate, controlled fury seeped into relationships, unnerving his mother and his clients. And then a close friend, who wouldn't take it anymore, ended his relationship with Neville. What was going on? Did he want to destroy his relationships?

And before too long, his beam of anger often focused on me. When I disagreed with him in conversation, he would put me down with intense, frigid wrath. Yelling would have been easier for me to understand than his cold fury.

There were many occasions when this showed up. One that stands out is when we were at a dinner party where I was discussing a topic that I was knowledgeable about, and he cut me off. Despite his complete ignorance of this subject, he told everyone how wrong I was and contradicted me. His meanness toward me embarrassed our host so much that she jumped in and changed the topic of conversation. On the drive home, he continued his rant about why I was wrong. I shut down, knowing the futility of disagreeing.

Over time and with greater frequency, Neville attacked all my opinions, insisting I was wrong. I didn't tell anyone about Neville's anger out of fear of his reprisal. Rather than turn to my family and friends, I began to withdraw from them. It was only years later that I realized Neville had been unrelenting in his verbal abuse of me.

I'm heading home with these harsh memories. Reflecting on the marriage, I realize how ready I was for that separation. But now, after the loss of Elizabeth and having left Olivia a thousand miles from home, I'm not at all ready for a new life on my own.

Chapter 25

Discovering Joy

Fall 2004 – Winter 2005

Before Olivia's college freshman year begins, Henry surprises me when he says, "I want to buy a condo in Charleston. I always said that if I ever have a vacation home, it would be there. Besides, I know that the transition to college is going to be hard for Olivia and you. We'd be able to visit her, see how she's doing, and if she needs some extra support, you'd be there for her."

I'm delighted that I'll be able to see Olivia more often. He quickly finds a condo about ten miles from downtown Charleston. It's light-filled and has views onto the Wando River, a mile-wide meandering waterway that ships and pleasure boats travel down from inland destinations to Charleston's harbor. Right away, he furnishes the condo.

A few weeks after Olivia starts her freshman year, she calls. Her excitement about college rings in her voice. "Mom, I like it here! I've made a new friend who lives next to my dorm room, and we have most of our meals together. She grew up in Charleston, and I'm getting to know her friends and fun places to hang out. And I really like my psychology teacher and my French lit class."

"I'm so happy for you!"

"The first weekend, we went to Foley Beach, swam, sunbathed, and played volleyball, but the last few weekends we've had rain. I was in my room a lot, and I don't really like my roommate." In a hushed voice, she whispers, "I'm glad I'm here, Mommy, but I miss you."

I try to cheer her up, telling her what's happening at my work, with our neighbors, and with our cat. "Lilly is back to bringing live chipmunks indoors. When I see one, I chase the little critter around the house and catch it. Remember when we used to laugh as we tried to catch them together?"

Olivia chuckles. "I do!"

I hang up the phone, happy to know that overall she's adjusting well to her first year away from home.

On our first visit to see Olivia, Henry and I participate in the college's parents' weekend. Olivia joins us for a campus tour, where we learn about the eighteenth- and nineteenth-century stucco and clapboard buildings at the historic core of the campus. After the tour, Olivia, Henry, and I stroll along palmetto tree-lined sidewalks and cobblestone streets in the lantern-lit retail district. We visit a Preservation Society historic house, then watch waves break on the Battery that once witnessed cannon balls launched from Union ships during the Civil War. We all fall under the spell of this city by the sea.

As we walk, college-aged men and women call out, "Hey, Olivia. How are you? Want to go to the beach on Saturday?"

"Sounds fun! I'll call you later." Her voice is upbeat. I'm thrilled to see her confidence.

It's not only enjoying time with Henry in his vacation home and seeing Olivia settle into her college life that brings me joy. It's also getting to know Henry's four children and his grandchildren. When they visit us in Charleston, their voices fill our condo with laughter and the antics of young children.

During the winter of Olivia's sophomore year, Henry's daughter Hannah and her family escape from the cold north winds, and the joyful sounds of frolicking children fill his condo. Many mornings, I take three-year-old Ben and one-year-old Chloe on walks next to the Wando River. They are delighted by the new sights and sounds around them.

One morning, just Ben and I go for a walk together. We explore at his pace, making our way to the riverbank along the sandy path coated with crushed seashells. We walk onto a wooden bridge that arches over a shallow creek. I pick up Ben so we can peer over the railing and search for watery mysteries together. It's low tide. We see impressions of raccoons' and egrets' feet pressed into the muddy banks and watch insects and thimble-sized crabs being swept in the outgoing tide.

As we stroll hand in hand, sunlit water sparkles and laps gently along the shore with a hypnotic, soothing sound. Palmetto trees with crosshatched, sinuous bark and spiky palm fronds root in sandy soil. Then Ben stops, stares up into the canopy of gnarled branches draped with Spanish moss, and takes a deep breath. He's no longer aware of me.

Ben whispers something, and I lean down to hear him.

"This is an enchanted forest."

Chapter 26

Awakening
Spring 2005

In Charleston my stronger self emerges, but often after I return home, I feel vulnerable again. It's the daily reminders that shake me. The way the afternoon sunlight fills Elizabeth's empty room, how the gossamer blossoms flutter on the weeping cherry tree, how my daughters' childhood photos sweep me back to earlier days. Over time, feelings of longing still wash over me, but they no longer disable me.

I discover that my worst setbacks are the unexpected ones. One day on my way home from work, I drive by the front lawn of the high school that Olivia attended. Girls lovely in their white robes and graduation caps and boys handsome in royal-blue gowns with matching mortarboards seize my attention. Then, I recognize one of Elizabeth's close friends, who was a classmate from kindergarten to eighth grade, a summer swim team buddy, and a favorite sleepover friend. I'm stunned. Elizabeth should have been graduating from high school today. She should have been radiant, dressed in her white gown and ready to celebrate with her friends. It's all wrong. I can't bear it. Tears blur my vision. I start to sob uncontrollably. I should pull over. Instead I speed home and bury my face in Elizabeth's pillow.

Despite these shattering setbacks, I know that I have to stay engaged with life. I don't want to slip back into despair. I push myself to get to the train each morning, apply myself at work each day, and accept some dinner invitations with Henry and friends at night. I listen to my protective voice too. Some evenings, I know when it's better to stay home, curl up, and read a book. I'm learning: Some days, I'll walk along with a steady gait. Other days, I'll stumble and trip. I'm beginning to accept that I'll be off-balance some days, and that's okay.

Henry and I return to Charleston for our vacations. It's comforting to see Olivia, hear news of her college courses and friends, and see her well adapted to the slower-paced Southern life.

Not only am I happy to spend time with Olivia and Henry, but I'm also drawn to the tidal rivers and often sit on sandy banks under the arching boughs of live oak trees. Here I feel embraced by the leafy boughs overhead and soothed by the sounds of water lapping on the sandy edge. Inhaling the salty moist air and feeling the sun warming my skin brings me into a dreamlike state. The afternoon sun casts a low, angled light that sparkles and glistens on the water. I close my eyes and listen. "Be quiet," whisper the softly rustling palms. "Be grateful," hints the shimmering sunlight. "Be free," says the ebb and flow of the river. Verses of joy flow through me. "I'm loved, I'm strong. I'm loved. I'm strong." Phrases I've never sung before. A new strength is being forged from the welding of my sorrow and joy, my loss and hope, my isolation and reengagement.

Near the tidal rivers and the sea, I remember family. My grandmother, who held me tenderly. My grandfather, whose upbeat ways and sparkling eyes cheered me. My mother, who loved to float in the salt water's buoyancy. And Elizabeth, whose aching body and mind were comforted by the infinite beauty of the sea. While on this Southern retreat, I wrote this poem.

Just Beyond Me

I swam last night.
A light softly lit the pool,
Palm fronds cast shadows on the grasses below.
I wandered home, body and mind relaxed.

This morning the rising sun reflected onto the river
and relayed shimmering messages on my living room wall.
It beckoned me outside;
I walked dreamily onto a dock in the wide-mouthed river.

I looked and listened for a long, long time.
The warm breezes stirred the river;
whitecaps crested and broke as they fell upon themselves.

The sun, now high above, shone upon the inland waterway,
but I turned my gaze away from the strong light
toward the deep blue passage to the sea.

Lizard-green grasses rose between the river
and the deep green swamp trees.
The wide, ambling river turned,
impeding my ability to see the sea.

But, I know it is there,
beyond my sight, but not beyond my imagination.

She, too, is in the realm that I cannot see;
Not lost, not gone, but just beyond me.

Now I know that she lives where the rivers meet the waters of eternity.

She lives just beyond my sight,
engaged, loving, laughing,
breathing in the sacred elements of God's divine mystery.

Chapter 27

Exploring

Summer 2005 – Summer 2007

My relationship with Henry grows even stronger, and we celebrate with an overseas adventure. We board a plane and land in Scotland. The arresting beauty of the craggy mountains, battered medieval fortresses, and dark-water lochs fill us with a sense of mystery. The ancient Scottish tales of rugged survival in these brooding highlands seems all too real.

After days of exploration, we pause to enjoy golf, one of our favorite activities. Henry is a skilled golfer, and I'm a high-handicap player. I strike the golf balls with vigor but don't wince if they stray. As an athlete, I love the challenge of improving my game. An added benefit of walking along the fairways is a revived feeling of well-being.

One day Henry and I play on a course in the medieval town of Beauly, in north-central Scotland. On the first hole, I hit my drive and watch the ball hook over a stone wall and bounce skyward as it hits a train track. Undaunted, I hit a mulligan, and this one travels over the fairway and lands a hundred yards from the pin. Henry lands far ahead near the green. As we walk down the hilly terrain, we have an expansive view of the surrounding farmland. Cows graze, and tractors plow vertical furrows in the adjacent fields. Sheep bleat, and a horse neighs as we approach.

On the sixteenth hole, we face a challenging par three. Fortunately, our tee shots land on the hilltop green. Pushing our carts, Henry and I huff and puff up the steep gravel-covered path, and we catch our breath at the top. Church bells begin to toll. It's Sunday evening at six o'clock, the hour of the Anglican Church's Evensong. The bells from two more church steeples join in, sounding like festive rings to announce a wedding. A deep sense of wonder fills me. Today would have been Elizabeth's nineteenth birthday. The joyful, exuberant chimes of the bells tell me that she is here . . . here with me in Beauly. Moments later, a few gray clouds and a gentle mist envelop us, and then a gusty wind sweeps them away. Beams of sunlight fall upon the fairways. Not one but two rainbows embrace the landscape.

After we return from Scotland, Hannah, four-year-old Ben, and two-year-old Chloe visit my home near Boston. We set off for an adventure to a secluded pond. We follow a path through a field bursting with white Queen Anne's lace, black-eyed Susans, purple asters, and goldenrod. The chirping sounds of crickets fill the air on this late afternoon August day. The path leads us into a glen of trees, and we rest in the cool of the shade. The children perk up and run ahead, leaving the woods behind. They dash into an opening that leads to the pond. The moment Ben feels the sand under his bare feet, he drops his backpack and towel and races toward water. "Look, Chloe! There are so many fish here. Come in and join me!" A few steps behind, Chloe joins the dash across the beach and splashes her feet in the refreshing water. Sunfish nibble at their ankles and cause shrieks of delight.

Not only is the walk to White's Pond filled with beauty, but the celadon-green, translucent water is so inviting. I step in and walk along the sandy bottom until the water is up to my chin. On the opposite side of the cove, evergreens line the water's edge and are bathed in the glow of the late-day sun.

Ben begins to dog paddle out into the cove as fast as he can. Hannah, ever watchful of her rambunctious boy, quickly calls him back to shore to put on his life vest. Once secure, he ventures even farther, paddling this way and that, gleeful in the joy of being afloat. Clipped into her life vest, Chloe follows suit. I swim by their sides and share in their excitement. "This is my favorite thing to do when we visit Pop and you!" yells Ben. "Mine too!" shouts Chloe.

Rolling over onto my back, I make slow circles with my arms and legs. Suddenly, I am swallowing gulps of water splashed by my mischievous companions. "I'm going to get you!" I bellow. The chase begins, and more high-spirited shouts echo across the water. Soon we're swimming side by side, squinting into the sun's reflection off the water, reveling in this end-of-summer day.

From his perch on a tree stump, Henry beams as he watches his daughter and grandchildren enjoying this family time. I know he's happy for me too. I've opened my heart to this young family, and their acceptance and love fills me with joy and gratitude.

An hour later, we dry the shivering children and help them pull on their T-shirts, shorts, and scuffed Crocs. As we begin our hike out, I turn to take one more look at this glorious pond that reminds me so much of the lake I swam in as a young camper in Maine. Chloe's little hand in mine, we walk along a path strewn with pine needles from the trees above. In time, the path leads us to the open field. Chloe stops to pick some colorful wildflowers and runs ahead to give them to her mother.

Henry and I join hands, watching the children as they skip and hop, stop and pick more flowers. A flock of Canada geese honking loudly flies overhead in perfect V formation. We all stop and look up to watch this end-of-summer passage.

Years ago, I could never have imagined this happiness.

Chapter 28
Tendrils of Love
Summer 2007

In the spring of Olivia's junior year, Henry proposes to me, and we plan a summer ceremony. On the morning of our wedding, Olivia and I drive to the historic clubhouse where our reception will be held and enter the dining room for breakfast. I look across at my firstborn child, grateful for our moment together. I reach over and hold Olivia's hand. "I love you, honey."

"I love you too, Mommy."

An hour later, when the bagpiper begins his melody, my father guides me down the aisle to my future husband. In the silence before the ceremony begins, Ben eagerly announces, "I have the ring!" Everyone chuckles at the enthusiasm of our four-year-old ring bearer.

Henry and I stand by the outdoor altar, holding hands. My sister Sarah and a close friend read two Bible passages. Then Olivia steps forward and in her clear voice sings, "What the World Needs Now Is Love Sweet Love." Olivia's voice fills the air with joy. When the song is over, I give her my bouquet of lilies and kiss her forehead. Then I turn toward Henry.

We look into each other's eyes, and I say our wedding vow:

This day is a moment
in the eternal rhythm of life;
we are part of this rhythm that has no beginning,
and has no ending.

One day I knew, and you did too,
that the rhythms of our lives are entwined.

Our love for each other is growing, flowing,
and as free as the waves cresting
and breaking upon the beach.

I promise to stand by your side,
to listen, to hold you,
to comfort you,
and share my life and family with you.

I promise to let your spirit be free—
to encourage you
and support you to become the person
who you were truly born to be.

I promise to speak with you
about my hopes, dreams, and worries,
and not to keep them inside.

And I promise
that when our twilight years arrive,
I will stay by your side.

Henry, however long forever is,
I want to be with you.

Henry responds,

Faith, with all my heart,
and all my love,
I join my life with yours.

We are pronounced husband and wife. We walk up a grassy hill arm in arm into the reception room adorned with arrangements of white lilies. I feel the warmth of the love of our families and closest friends. I hold Henry tightly as we dance to "The Way You Look Tonight." His returning embrace promises love, security, and strength for the years ahead.

The day after our wedding, Henry and I fly to Bermuda. I feel rested, comforted, loved. For the first time in years, I know that I am loved for who I am.

During our honeymoon, while enjoying the colors of the verdant lawns, pink sandy beaches, and turquoise sea, I think of Elizabeth's Make-A-Wish trip on this tropical island. I often just close my eyes and remember her floating on a raft in the lagoon, hear her chatter with Olivia and Annie, and see her gazing up at the stars at night. Here she was at peace.

I hear her gentle voice and see the twinkle in her eyes. I feel her arms wrapped around my neck when I kissed her good night. When I remember her now, I'm released from my disabling grief.

In this new beginning, love has led me, ever so gently, to a safe and peaceful place where I can become the woman I'm longing to be.

Part 3
"Destiny"

Years ago, life clobbered me,
but a stubborn part of me would not give up.

Now, I am free to choose my destiny.
It is up to me.

Chapter 29

Celebrations

Summer 2008

Henry and I are sitting under the sweeping branches of a centuries-old live oak tree. The moss dangling from its branches sways in the breeze. The venerable two-hundred-year-old courtyard, the central gathering place of Olivia's college, surrounds us. We're facing an impressive two-story administration building with a columned façade modeled after the Greek Parthenon. With its majestic symmetry and reverence to the wisdom of the ancient Greeks, one feels the past presence of learned people who gathered in this peaceful place.

Instead of its usual quiet hush, the courtyard is bustling today with hundreds of guests finding their ways to chairs. They're eager to locate a good view from which to watch their daughter or son cross the podium and graduate with the class of 2008. To my right, my sister Sarah; her husband, Stephen; and my niece, Robin, banter. Everyone is caught up in the excitement of the day. We're lucky to have an unobstructed view so we will be able to see the students receiving their diplomas.

Henry and I are perched on the edge of our chairs in anticipation. Commencement begins with a ceremonial speech by the president of the college. Soon, male students clad in maroon robes and female students wearing white dresses and carrying red roses cross the stage ahead of us. One by one they shake hands with the gathered college leadership, receive their diplomas, and wave to the cheering audience. My eyes are fixed on the entrance to the stage. Close to a thousand students are graduating from the College of Sciences, so my wait is lengthy, but I'm as excited as the students are for this grand occasion. One hour later, Olivia confidently strides onto the center of the stage in her white cotton dress with a maroon ribbon and gold medallion draped around her neck. Her golden hair falls over one shoulder. Even from the distance, I can see her radiant smile. She's graduating with high honors. She has made it. Waves of gratitude rush over me. This is the greatest gift that Olivia could have given me.

Six months before Olivia's graduation, Henry and I planned a celebration because our youngest daughters were approaching major adult milestones. Lucy, my twenty-two-year-old stepdaughter, would be receiving a graduate degree in art, and Olivia would be receiving a bachelor's degree in psychology. We were also aware that while Henry and I were dating, Lucy and Olivia lived in different parts of the country, and even after our wedding, their paths rarely crossed. We hoped that during a vacation on a tropical island, not only would they get to know each other but they'd have fun together too.

Four weeks after Olivia's graduation, Henry, Lucy, Olivia, and I fly to a resort in Barbados. We step from our air-conditioned car into warm and balmy air. We're greeted and guided to the double cabana where we'll stay. Inside there's a terracotta tile entry and a room painted in pastel yellows and greens. Light pours in through oversized windows. A ceiling fan purrs overhead. We have duplicate rooms on either side of a shared wall. That evening we walk to the open and airy dining area that has no walls but instead has trellises intertwined with flowering vines. We'll love eating al fresco! Not only are we thrilled with our cabanas and the open dining area, but the inviting sea is mere steps away.

I swim at least four times a day: before breakfast, late morning, midafternoon, and again in the early evening. I float in the buoyant turquoise water, cradled by the gentle rise and fall of the waves. I gaze at the billowing clouds above. All will be well in this tropical paradise.

One morning we decide to go waterskiing. The young men available to drive the boat race to help us—our beautiful, fun-loving daughters are quite a draw! Everyone decides that I should waterski first. I'm not convinced. I haven't been waterskiing since I was eleven, but realizing that I might never have this opportunity again, I put on my life vest, plunge into the sea, and slide on my skis. The young driver calls out, "Are you ready? Bend your legs. Keep your arms straight! Let the power of the boat pull you out of the water." I repeat these commands over and over in my mind as the engine speed picks up. The line I'm holding goes taut, and suddenly I'm up! I stay in the smooth part of the wake, not daring to test my strength by maneuvering from side to side. It's thrilling! Lucy shouts, "Go, Faith!" Olivia hollers, "Yeah, Mommy!" The wind whistles past my ears, my arms grow tired, but I hold tightly to the rope. I feel free and strong, the way I felt as a child waterskiing at summer camp so long ago.

Lucy is next. She has never been waterskiing but she's an expert snowboarder, and I have no doubt she'll succeed. She shouts, "Ready!" The engine roars, and she's up! Soon, she's waterskiing in and out of the wake gracefully, as if she has waterskied for years. Then it's Olivia's turn. She's only been on a kneeboard once, as a child, so this will be a challenge. Six times the engine roars, the line goes taut, but she careens off-balance and into the water. Not one to give up, on her seventh try she succeeds and stands up. Olivia beams.

Each day brings a new adventure. We set sail on a captained

catamaran in search of green sea turtles. Olivia and I are sitting on the canvas that stretches between the two long runners of the sailboat. We hit our first large wave at high speed with spraying water soaking us, and we laugh with surprise and sheer exuberance. Anchoring at a coral reef, we don snorkels and masks and jump into aquamarine waters. I motion to Olivia and Lucy to look on the starboard side of the boat, where a giant sea turtle is slowly swimming. Soon, we are thrilled to see several sea turtles swimming under and around us. Despite being three to four feet in length, they swim as gracefully as the much smaller fish that pass by us. The sea turtles even allow us to swim within a few feet of them before, in one majestic sweep, their giant flippers swiftly move them to a new location. Thirty minutes later, the captain pulls up anchor and sets his course for a different coral reef. After we arrive, and our snorkels and masks are in place, the captain hands us crackers and tells us to crumble them into the sea and then jump in. Within minutes, the waters are churning with brightly colored fish. My heart is pounding hard as I look through my mask and see flashes of blue, green, orange, and yellow swirling around me. At the end of the day, we return sun-kissed, tired, and happy. That night, Henry asks Olivia which adventure she'd like to go on tomorrow, and she replies, "Horseback riding by the sea!"

The following day, a well-worn van picks us up, and we drive to a rural and less populated part of the island. About thirty minutes later, the van sputters, and then the engine gives out completely. Our only option in this remote area is to get out, push the van downhill, and hope the driver can kick-start the engine. After we push the van for a stretch, the engine engages, and we run breathlessly after it. We jump in laughing and continue on our journey. We arrive at a down-at-the-heels riding stable, where a friendly older woman greets us.

Before we set off on our horses, Lucy puts her arm around Olivia, and I take a photograph of them—smiling, confident, and happy with their new friendship. We mount our horses and ride single file through a dense forest. The stable dogs that moments ago had lain lazily in the yard now run alongside us, barking excitedly. They dash between the horses with surprising agility. As the horses move slowly uphill, the path begins to widen, and soon we have a panoramic view of small farmland plots and beyond to the eastern coast of the island. Even from a distance, this coastline, unlike the southwest coast where we are staying, looks wild and untamed. The beach, devoid of houses or people, extends for miles. Large ocean swells and whitecaps play on the tumultuous surface of the sea.

Slowly we descend the steepest part of the trail, aware of the low roar of the ocean. All at once the wind picks up, and it begins to rain. This is no ordinary summer shower but a heavy tropical downpour. The air is turbulent, the rains pelting, the winds whipping around me. Rain pours off my riding helmet in heavy streams and cascades onto my lap. My drenched clothes cling to me. A thrilling, exhilarating sensation swells up in me. A voice inside me shouts, "Be free, explore, revel in this adventure." I wonder, if I had lived a hundred years ago, would I have been brave enough to travel to a Caribbean island and leave behind the world I grew up in? Or would I have ventured across the American West in a wagon train and settled on an unexplored coast? A fiery spirit within me burns to be set free: free to explore, to experience new places, other cultures, and new ways of living. This sensation is exhilarating.

The rain tapers to a light mist, and then it ceases. The roar of the ocean grows louder as we approach the beach. Crashing waves meet the shoreline and dissolve into foam. As I ride along the beach, warm, humid air fills my lungs, and the salty spray clings to my body. I move with the hypnotic motion of my horse's swaying body and gaze out to the sea. Completely at ease, I loosen the reins to let my horse lead me. I lean forward and hug the neck of my old mare, thanking her for carrying me on such an unforgettable journey.

On our last day in Barbados, Henry, Olivia, and I are perusing the breakfast menu when our waiter asks if there will be a fourth person joining us. Olivia responds, "Yes, my sister will be here soon." My heart swells at her brief reply.

Chapter 30

Past and Present

Fall – Winter 2008

Despite our uplifting vacation in Barbados, I have difficulty returning to life at home, perhaps because my house is filled with so many memories. In the middle of the night, I'm flooded with nightmares, seeing Elizabeth pale and weak, seeing shadowy figures move around her bed at night, and then searching frantically for Elizabeth but not being able to find her. I wake up with a jolt. I will myself to remember happier times from when my daughters were young—when we baked together, played with their hamsters, or cuddled on the sofa while watching a movie. If those memories don't calm my racing mind, I say the Buddhist prayer of lovingkindness again and again. Its gentle mantra soothes me.

By day, I fare better. I've launched myself into a new career as the director of communication at a school for children with dyslexia. I'm proud to be part of a community focused on improving the skills and well-being of students who have a learning disability. I write stories for the school's magazine that feature achievements of the students and the highly trained faculty. I craft admissions materials, development magazines, and news for the school's website. This career suits me.

Being with children every day has its risks for me too. One morning I'm walking in a stairwell on my way to a meeting and I hear a repetitive *beep, beep, beep*. The sound keeps going on and on, and I find myself shaking. I'm transported back to the hospital, hearing the *beep, beep, beep* set off when Elizabeth's IV bag was empty. Tears well up in my eyes. I take deep breaths to steady myself and then realize that the beeping sound is coming from a malfunctioning fax machine in the office I'm walking past.

One other time when the past catapults into the present is on the day before the eighth-grade graduation. Parents are gathered on the lawn, talking eagerly about their family's summer plans and where their son or daughter will be going to school in the fall. I don't see it coming. All of a sudden, I'm clobbered by the memory of Elizabeth's eighth-grade graduation. I see her crossing the stage, frail and thin, and reaching out for her diploma. I see her unexpected radiant smile as she holds up her diploma. My heart aches as I remember this moment, and I can't hold back the tears. How long will this happen? How many times will I be jarred by the past? Maybe it will happen forever.

The seasons change, and my days do too. Some days are filled with writing deadlines at school, others with walks with friends or visits with family. I join a choir and feel comforted by being in church again. One morning at church, a friend asks me if Henry and I will have children. To his surprise I immediately reply, "No, but we'll have puppies!" Within a month of this conversation, I connect with a friend who is a breeder of Goldendoodles. Soon after, we bring home nine-week-old Charlie. He is sandy colored with enormous paws and a gentle personality. We're thrilled to have him as a part of our family. He adds a dimension of joy and rambunctiousness that makes us laugh. By the time he is twelve months old, he's an energetic seventy-pound pup.

One of my favorite places to walk Charlie is at an old farm lined by stone walls, crossed by a brook, and teeming with chipmunks, deer, and turkeys. On a cold winter morning, Charlie and I walk across an abandoned apple orchard at the farm. The weathered apple trees bend, burdened with the coating of ice from the previous night's storm. Fields of frozen snow reflect the pale blue sky above. The arctic air takes my breath away. Charlie bounds ahead of me, running exuberantly over the frozen fields. He stops at a frozen pile of manure; his search for pungent odors is insatiable. He rears up like a horse, arches his back, and then pounces forward, his front legs breaking through the icy crust. Enthusiastically, he discovers what is underneath, breathes in its pungent delights, and then runs down the trail ahead.

Walking over the crusted, icy surface, I frequently break through and sink into the snow below. I walk slowly, crunching my way across the field and onto the trail leading into the woods. We play a favorite game: Charlie runs ahead but always stops and looks back at me. I crouch down and then jump into the air. He barrels back toward me and, at the last minute, runs around me in a high-speed circle. He bounds ahead, stops, looks back, and we do it all over again. Only the sounds of Charlie's high-speed gallop and my footsteps permeate this quiet morning.

Thank heavens for Charlie's need for exercise. When we explore the town's many conservation trails, I'm pulled away from my computer and my list of "to dos." Instead I focus on the differences between evergreen and deciduous trees, the crunch of the leaves or ice under my feet, the woodpecker's *rat-a-tat-tat* tapping sounds echoing through the forest, and the flash of a long, white, wooly tail as deer bound nearby. All is well here. These trails, these forests are welcoming. I never feel alone when walking under the forest's canopy or across open fields. Nature embraces me. Its gentle presence flows through and around me. The natural world gives me the gift of peace and belonging.

Chapter 31
Early Morning
Winter 2009

When I was in my early to midforties and my world was bleak, I never could have anticipated that I would have the joy of spending time with young children so soon after Elizabeth died. It would have seemed like an impossible dream. I wish Elizabeth could see me now playing with Ben, age five, and Chloe, age three. Elizabeth would have been beaming because she knew how much joy children bring to me. I would have loved sharing my adventures with her.

One weekend while Ben and Chloe's parents are away, Henry and I take care of them. In the early morning, I hear the patter of light footsteps on the floor above me. As I lie in bed, I hear Chloe walking carefully down the stairs and across the living room floor. She approaches our bed quietly and slips in next to me. She whispers, "Will Pop be a monster in the playhouse today?"

"Would you like him to be a monster?"

"Yes!"

The morning light is gray, and everyone else is still sleeping. It's too early to get up, so I lie still, and Chloe wiggles closer to me. "How is your baby doll, Lucy?" I whisper.

"She is sleeping."

"Oh. Good."

I drift back to sleep. Moments later I hear the sound of Chloe sucking her thumb, inches away from my ear. I haven't woken to this sweet sound in many years.

A half hour later, we have another visitor. Ben climbs up on the bed and flops down enthusiastically between Pop and me. He has brought his favorite toy, a plastic claw, and soon he is grabbing sheets, pillowcases, anything in its path. Exuberant about the prospect of a new day, he whispers story after story about his mom, his toolbox with a "real" hammer, his new wheelbarrow, and his favorite headband that has a headlight attached. He bounds off the bed, slips on the headband, and gives us a demonstration in the predawn light.

Chloe is sleeping soundly, so we slip quietly out of bed. Shackleton, their nine-year-old lab, slaps her tail enthusiastically on the wooden floors. This is my clue that she is ready for her kibble. Ben climbs onto his stool at the kitchen counter and greets his fighting fish in the fish bowl. He shakes in a little fish food and watches his prize possession carefully. He then asks the fish to watch him while he's having his breakfast. What a gift to start the day with these affectionate, imaginative children.

Later in the morning, we visit an art studio, where we help Ben and Chloe make frogs out of felt and then decorate them with multicolored sequins. Chloe also loves painting at the easel. She chooses some bright colors and paints with abandon. Ben joins a group of young boys who are squirting spray paint at figures drawn on the wall. This activity is allowed, and even encouraged, but squirting another child is not. Within minutes one boy is crying, and Ben looks at me with a mischievous grin as if to say, *I didn't do it!*

At noon, we bundle up the children and walk outside to a cool, blustery spring day. Ben and Chloe are hungry and grumpy, so we stop at a grocery store, where I buy crackers, creamy peanut butter, grape jelly, and some juice boxes. We drive to a coastal state park. The children jump out of the car and run to the swing set in a central grassy area. But Ben quickly returns because he has run out of energy. He needs his lunch. A particular eater, he only eats special foods that his mom makes for him. But today, in a pinch, I infuse some magic into his meal.

"Would you like to eat some pirate snacks?" I ask.

"What are those?" Ben responds.

I give him a cracker layered with peanut butter and jelly.

"Is this what pirates eat?"

"Yes!"

Happily, he gobbles down his pirate food, drinks his juice, and then runs back to the playground. Chloe joins us, and after finishing her lunch, she follows Ben to the playground. We play together with Pop until everyone is tired, and we head back home.

At dinner that evening, I ask Chloe what her favorite part of the day was, expecting her to say making the felt frogs or playing on the swings. But instead, she looks me straight in the eyes and says, "Being with Pop and you."

Six months later, Pop, Ben, Chloe, and I are sitting on a wooden bench in a train that runs along the coast of Casco Bay.

"This is a diesel engine train, Faith."

"How do you know that, Ben?"

"Because it has a horn; a train with a steam engine has a whistle."

Ben loves trains, hence this morning's special adventure. We've stepped aboard a refurbished locomotive train built in 1882 that was designed to carry passengers from Portland, Maine, to Montreal along the Atlantic & St. Lawrence Railroad. Today the locomotive follows a much shorter route along the Portland coastline.

Looking out the window, I see fathers and sons throwing Frisbees, people walking along the rocky beach, lovers lying side by side on the grassy embankment, and dozens of small sailboats on Casco Bay.

Unlike most days in November, today is balmy and sunny. Ben is wiggling with excitement. The horn sounds, and Ben beams. Chloe nestles close to me, but Ben sits apart, absorbed in the journey.

Ben and Chloe's parents, Will and Hannah, are away for the weekend. They are always incredibly appreciative when we look after their children and give them some "off-duty" time, but honestly, they are giving a gift to Henry and me. It is a blessing to spend uninterrupted time with Ben and Chloe, making pancakes in the morning, embarking on daytime adventures, and reading stories to them by the fire at night.

The following morning, Ben crawls onto our bed before dawn, much earlier than his normal seven thirty wake-up time. Needing more rest before the day begins, Henry and I pretend to be asleep. But that doesn't deter Ben from playing with his Old MacDonald tractor that beeps and produces the sounds of sheep baaing and horses neighing. An hour later I ask, "Honey, why did you wake up so early this morning?"

Ben replies, "Because I want to spend more special time with you and Pop."

Chapter 32

Giving Thanks
Summer – Fall 2009

The year after Olivia graduates from college, she stays in Charleston and works as a server in a high-end restaurant. One day while I am visiting, she enthusiastically tells me that she'd like to pursue a career as a speech and language pathologist. She'll need a graduate degree, so one month later, Olivia and I drive north for an interview at a university in Knoxville. She will meet with the head of the audiology and speech pathology department and with a professor who teaches audiology courses.

Dr. Gray welcomes us warmly. She tells us that this program specializes in the rehabilitation of young children with cochlear implants. This is exactly the area that Olivia wants to specialize in. My daughter's face lights up as she and Dr. Gray engage in a lively conversation. When Dr. Gray's assistant enters the room to let her know that her noon conference call is underway, Dr. Gray replies, "Please tell them that I'll join the conversation later." She turns and gives Olivia her full attention.

At the end of the hour, Dr. Gray tells Olivia that she could apply for enrollment in the program beginning in mid-August. After exchanging warm good-byes, Olivia meets with the audiology professor, and then we stop by the office of another. This professor asks Olivia where she is living now. Olivia replies, "Well, all my worldly goods are packed in two cars, and we are heading to my parents' home in Boston." The professor pauses and then says, "Well, you could just stay."

Olivia beams.

After Olivia moves to Knoxville for her graduate program, I fly there to spend Thanksgiving with her. Olivia and I are sitting on a friend's balcony, welcoming the warmth of the late afternoon sun as we watch the Tennessee River. It flows effortlessly, sparkling in the sunlight, dotted here and there by a few boats. I ask Olivia about her courses. She replies that she is enjoying them. I'm so proud of her when she tells me that she is getting straight As. She tells me about her new friends and new places nearby that she likes to visit. Later we take Maggie, her two-year-old Goldendoodle, for a long walk in a nearby park.

On Thanksgiving morning, Olivia is not feeling well enough to go out for lunch, and a kind neighbor brings us a meal of sliced turkey, mashed potatoes, cranberry relish, green beans, and gravy. We enjoy it in Olivia's apartment. I feel especially close to her on this quiet holiday. After lunch, we watch *Some Like It Hot*, and we laugh a lot.

After lunch, I take Maggie for a walk. She prances in front of me with her head and tail held high, as if to say, "I'm walking with my pack leader today. Aren't I lucky?" We walk along a pedestrian bridge that crosses over a busy city street. On the other side is the World's Fair Park built in Knoxville in 1981. For this grand fair, the city created a welcoming park with pedestrian paths, grassy fields to host events, and an outdoor amphitheater covered by three overlapping canvas structures resembling the sails of a ship. At the far edge of the amphitheater, a tranquil pond shimmers in the sunlight.

We continue our walk in the park, and soon we are under the

arches of a second pedestrian bridge. I pause and draw in my breath. Embedded in the walls are three large displays of handmade tiles honoring "Cancer Survival Days" from the late 1990s. I read on the tiled walls, "Our little Angel, Elizabeth Collier, May 29, 1994," "Whatever Happens I Cannot Fail—Dian, May 1998," "In Memory of Mary Alice Bates—September 10, 1984," "Survive, Hope, Laugh, Love—That Is Life." These are a few of the dozens of messages on the walls in front of me. I'm not prepared for the sudden grip of grief that seizes me. *Elizabeth, Elizabeth, Elizabeth, why were you taken from me? I want you to be here, to see your sister in graduate school, to walk with me in this park, to talk with me the way we used to, to know my new husband is Henry.* I read more messages with my heart pounding. Why does cancer shatter so many, many lives?

Minutes later, I feel Maggie tugging on the leash, and I turn away from the display. Soon Maggie pulls me in the direction of the playing field. The wide green expanse of grass excites her, and she begins to run full speed around me in circles. I twirl to follow her and then start to run. I'm breathless by the time we reach the far end of the field. She has drawn me away from the wall of suffering and into the world of the living. As I pause, my tears dry, and my heart stops pounding. We stroll back to Olivia's apartment.

The following day, Olivia and I drive to a community called Cherokee about five miles from downtown Knoxville. The meandering road is lined by handsome houses made of stucco, brick, and stone. I catch glimpses of the Tennessee River behind them. After a couple of miles, we turn off the road and into a parking lot next to the river. Maggie starts whining and then barks excitedly after she realizes where we've stopped. This is her favorite place to explore.

The air is mild, the sun is shining, and a slight breeze rustles six-foot-tall grasses lining the bank of the Tennessee River. Maggie loves to bound through the grasses before jumping into the river, where she laps up a cool drink. She paddles around for a few minutes, finds a place to climb out, and then jumps over the rocks and onto the well-worn path near the river's edge. Olivia and I share stories as we walk along the path.

The light glistens on the river, and I'm drawn to the water's edge. As I pause there quietly, my body absorbs the warmth of this day. A profound sense of peace and well-being swells up in me. Silently, I say a prayer of thanksgiving.

Chapter 33
Pain and Joy
Spring – Fall 2010

My life turns upside down the following winter. After six weeks of excruciating back pain that will not abate and severe shooting pain running down my right leg, I'm in agony. Physical therapy has only made my condition worse. After I wake up one morning, I can't even move without screaming. Sobbing, I call my father and ask him for the name of the neurosurgeon who operated on my mother. Dr. Adams, he tells me, and says that he'll call him tomorrow morning after the office opens. But I utter, "I know it's early Sunday morning, but I can't wait even one more day. I need to go to the hospital now!" My father says that he'll call the neurosurgeon right away. Unable to walk upright, I crawl to the car. I scream as Henry lifts me into the back seat. I lie there miserable as Henry drives me to the hospital. On the way, I pray the Buddhist prayer of lovingkindness to calm me. I pray that I will be admitted to the emergency room and into the hospital. I pray that Dr. Adams will operate.

Henry pulls into the ER parking area of a Boston hospital and gets help. Two EMTs slide a board under me in the back seat. I holler and shout profanities. Once out of the car, I am slid onto a gurney and brought into the ER. I'm seen by an ER doctor immediately. To my dismay, he tells me that he can give me painkillers, but he can't do more than that today. He says I have to have an appointment with a neurosurgeon, who can then schedule an operation. I can't believe it. I shout, "But I can't move without screaming! I can't get back into my car. I can't bear this pain!"

The ER doctor leaves the room where I'm lying, and I overhear a conversation going on outside the door. Moments later, a different doctor walks in. "Hi, I'm Dr. Adams's intern. We're expecting you. Tell me what's going on." Five minutes later, Dr. Adams walks in. "Hi, Faith. When I was making my hospital rounds this morning, I received the call from your father. You'll have an MRI today, and if you have a herniated disk, I'll operate within a few days. After I remove the disc that is pushing into your spinal canal, you'll feel much better." His manner is kind. His words are like manna from heaven.

I'm given an IV with painkillers, and Henry holds my hand as we wait for my MRI to be scheduled. Now that the rush is over, I look around my room, at the IV pole, and watch the fluid drip, drip, drip down the tube and into my vein. I listen to a woman crying, a man shouting, and the commotion outside my room. Henry whispers soothing words to me. An hour later, after my MRI, I'm wheeled into a room on Ellison 12, six floors below where Elizabeth and I stayed nearly nine years ago. My room looks onto the Charles River as Elizabeth's rooms frequently did. I'm relieved to be here, but being in a room that mirrors Elizabeth's is almost unbearable.

The following morning, Dr. Adams operates. In the days that follow as I'm in and out of a drugged state, I remember watching Elizabeth when she was too weak to even swallow a spoonful of applesauce, and as her hair, streaked with summer highlights, fell in clumps onto her sheets. I remember the nights when I could not sleep, when I sat on the edge of her hospital bed, held her hand, and stroked her soft cheeks. I remember how desolate I felt at night, how I willed myself to be strong during the days.

I'm in a dreadful state. Following the surgery, the shooting pain down my right leg is gone, but new pain caused by the deep incisions is excruciating. The pain medications are so strong I even hallucinate. I imagine that I'm sitting in a sunny outdoor dining area like the one in Barbados. My unconscious mind is certainly trying to escape my hospital surroundings!

The week I spend in the hospital only feels like a few days. Soon, I'm home again, and Henry is nursing me. While I'm grateful for his help with my medical care, he can't help my downward emotional slide. I'm an athlete, and it's so hard for me to be bedridden. I try each day to walk a few more steps, to eat a little more food, to take less medication. Even though Henry is present during many of the days, I miss walking, swimming, and playing tennis with my friends. Recovering for weeks and weeks at home and in bed is so isolating.

A month later, to cheer me up, Hannah, Ben, and Chloe come to visit during their spring vacation. Their gentle hugs and laughter lighten my otherwise morose mood. On the second day of their visit, Henry, Hannah, Ben, and Chloe say good-bye and set off for Concord to watch the local Patriots' Day festivities. I can imagine them watching minutemen from Acton, Concord, and Lincoln march in formation, the bands from local schools marching and playing rousing tunes, and cannon-bearing carriages drawn by Clydesdale horses parading. But instead of watching these activities as I have for years, I'm in my bed sobbing.

A few hours later, Chloe and Ben return home from the parade with balloons in hand. Ben is particularly proud of his Transformers balloon. They are boisterous, and it takes a while for Hannah to settle them down and give them lunch and a bath. As Hannah combs her daughter's fine blonde hair, Chloe asks, "Mommy, when you are done, can I snuggle with Faith?"

Chloe picks out her favorite picture books and crawls under the flannel covers near me. A few minutes into the second story, I pause, and inches away from my ear, I hear her gently sucking her thumb as she drifts off to sleep. What comfort these children bring to me.

As the weeks go by, I begin to think differently about suffering. I read books about grieving and healing and suffering and recovering. The words of the Buddhist nun Pema Chödrön stay with me and offer a new beginning: "On a very basic level all beings think that they should be happy. When life becomes difficult or painful, we feel that something has gone wrong. According to Buddhist teachings, difficulty is inevitable in human life . . . we cannot escape the reality of death . . . [or] the realities of aging, of illness . . . or the sorrow at losing what you love." Chödrön points out that we are somehow conditioned to believe that we do not deserve our unhappiness; we think it unfair. "In reality," Chödrön continues, "when you feel depressed, lonely, betrayed, or [have] any unwanted feelings, this is an important moment on the spiritual path. This is where real transformation can take place."[1]

I try to take a few tentative steps in this direction in my daily thoughts. I imagine my sorrow and pain reshaping from dark gray storm clouds that give way to light cumulous clouds. Now I begin to understand that I need to stay with my pain, to live through the bleak stormy days, and to know that better days will come my way.

In June, three months after my surgery, Henry and I gather with family and close friends to witness Lucy and her fiancé, Keith, say their wedding vows. Henry chokes up. He's happy for Lucy and Keith, but he knows that a marriage brings a sea change in a father–daughter relationship. From now on, Lucy will first turn to Keith for help in navigating life's journey. In the party following the ceremony, rousing applause follows many toasts. Guests swirl on the dance floor. All too soon, the bride and groom leave for their honeymoon. The sunny and warm summer day has given way to a moonlit night. Henry and I hold hands and look at the moonlight reflecting on the sea in front of us. It's been a glorious wedding.

As I continue to heal, I'm able to return to work, to swimming and walking with friends. Other sports, like tennis, will have to wait until my back is completely recovered from the surgery. My mood improves with the joy of being able to be engaged in life again. To celebrate my new lease on life, Henry and I return to Pompano Beach, the lovely Bermudian resort by the sea where we spent our honeymoon. During the day, we're drawn to the turquoise waters and the pink beaches; at night the balmy evening air soothes us while the cicadas serenade. One night after dinner, we walk hand in hand along a moonlit path. A gentle breeze rustles my pale pink-and-gray silk dress. We listen to the waves cascading into the volcanic rocks that line the shoreline below us. Henry and I pause and hold each other in a tight embrace.

Bermuda's beauty draws me into a sense of well-being. When immersed in a world of yellow, pink, and green tropical flora, pastel houses, azure-blue skies, and coral-pink beaches, how can I not feel the deep harmony that emanates from such beauty? One morning we join four other guests and set sail on a boat with a veteran skipper. The skipper decides to sail the boat in the protected inland harbor rather than along the windy south shoreline. The wind is breezy, the clouds are few, and we sail in and out of small coves and around numerous private islands scattered in the harbor. We see three-story yellow, pink, and pale blue mansions, their immaculately mowed lawns garnished with private docks. We also see smaller houses, painted brightly with colors of sunflower yellow, lime green, or cornflower blue, dotting the edges of the harbor's shoreline. Whether a mansion or a humble house, the ubiquitous whitewashed roofs brightly reflect the sun's rays.

We sail into a quiet cove and set anchor. Unable to resist the lure of the sparkling water, I dive overboard. As I swim the breaststroke, my arms and legs glide effortlessly. In the shallow waters, I dive under the surface and see clusters of pink coral with pastel-colored fish sucking at them. The fish scatter wildly as I approach. Leaving the underwater world, I return to the surface, the sunlight reflecting brightly in front of me. I float freely on my back, arms and legs extended like a starfish. A deep peace blooms inside me.

The school year begins again, and I accelerate into high gear at work. Writing news for the website, articles for the school magazine, and development and admissions brochures fills my days and some of my nights too. I'm happy to see the children skipping down the halls, learning in the classrooms, and playing sports on the fields. But I'm upset that after sitting at my desk for only thirty minutes, a gnawing back pain interrupts my concentration. Within weeks, I'm hobbling down hallways and up stairs, and, unable to sit, I try working at a standing desk. Nothing abates my discomfort. One evening in late November, I'm hobbling at home and an acute, sharp pain drops me to the ground. I can't move without screaming. I call my doctor, and she tells me to go to the ER. An intern for my neurosurgeon will be waiting for me.

Within the hour, I'm on a stretcher being wheeled into the ER. The MRI confirms that I have a herniated disk that is pressing on my spinal cord. Dr. Adams arrives and tells me that he will operate as soon as he can secure an operating room.

Once again, I'm back in a room overlooking the Charles River. I start sobbing. I don't want to be here again. I'm hurting, and I've become anxious too. I'm given a cocktail of oxycodone and Ativan. Soon, I'm groggy and teary. In the middle of the night, I wake up in excruciating pain. The nurse gives me another dose of painkillers,

and I doze off. The next day in the predawn light, Dr. Adams walks
into my room and says that he will operate on me that day. I ask,
"When?" He replies, "Right now!" I'm elated. More medication is
pumped into my IV. I start to pray but conk out instead.

My surgery is over. I sleep most of the first day of recovery. The following day is Thanksgiving. I'm groggy, teary, and unable to find
any comfortable position in my hospital bed. Nurses come and go,
Dr. Adams visits, but all I want is to be at home, to be celebrating
Thanksgiving with my family, but I can't even walk six steps to the
bathroom. I fall in and out of a drugged sleep for days. After one
week, I return home. I never ever want to go through lumbar spine
surgery again.

The first month of my recovery is tough, and I recognize that I'm
depressed. The pain medications have contributed to my depression,
as well as the sadness I feel around Christmas and the new year.
This year as the holiday tunes take over the radio stations, and as
I watch cars go by with Christmas trees tied on top, I can't get into
the holiday spirit. I decide that another retreat at the peaceful monastery might restore me. On the day of my planned departure, mac-
aroon-size snowflakes are cascading to the ground, adding six more
inches to this year's already record snowfall. It's not safe to drive to
the monastery, so instead, I put on my warmest down coat, gloves,
and hat and walk silently along our snow-covered, unplowed street.
The heavy snowfall muffles the sound of passing cars on the road
nearby. I only hear the squeak of my boots as they press on clumps
of snow. Returning to my house, I find a tennis ball and play with
Charlie. Our dog, now fully grown, stands three feet tall and has fur
the color of wheat ale with amber patches on his chest and beard. His
nose, dusted with snow, is the color of hot chocolate. I throw the ball;
Charlie bounds through the deep snow and grabs the ball, and then

I wrestle it from his mouth. I throw the ball again, and he snuffles in the snow until he finds it. We repeat our playful game until I'm chilled.

Charlie has brought a joy into our lives that few but the most ardent animal lovers would understand. At night while I watch TV or read on the sofa, he rests his head on my chest; his warm breaths fall gently on my face. Having Charlie by my side comforts me. Years before Elizabeth died, a friend once told me, "Dogs fill the holes inside us." Now, I know this is true.

The next day, after the snowstorm abates, I drive to the monastery. The stone walls lining the roads are piled high with snow. Birch trees bend under the weight of the snow clinging to them. The woodland paths and fields are blanketed with three-foot-deep snow. The first night while I'm driving from my hermitage to the main house for dinner, only a few feet in front of me a deer leaps over one stone wall, pauses, looks into the headlights, and then leaps over the far wall. As I am thinking, *When there is one deer, there are always two*, a buck with an impressive rack of antlers bounds over the stone wall closest to me, glides across the road, and then leaps over the far stone wall and into the darkness. It's magical.

The days, far away from the bustle of daily life, are peaceful. I rest and write in the quiet hermitage and attend chapel services. On the last day of my stay, I watch, once more, the setting sun. A congregation of clouds lights up, displaying colors of lilac, raspberry, bright copper, and golden tangerine. *Here* I am in the presence of a radiant Being.

Chapter 34
The Unexpected
Fall 2011 – Summer 2012

Olivia is in her second year of the Speech-Language Pathology master's degree program. During the late spring and summer months, she takes on a full schedule of classes and a practicum at a local clinic where children with hearing loss receive medical care and speech therapy. In a noticeable change, Olivia does not answer my calls. I am not sure if she is on a path to more independence or if she is struggling in graduate school but does not want me to know. During the next month, Olivia's silence unnerves me. She's still not responding to my attempts to reach her.

One morning in late September, Olivia calls me while I'm at work. "I'm so unhappy here. I know you'll be so disappointed, Mommy, but I have to leave." Between her sobs, Olivia continues, "I can't concentrate. I can't do my work. I can't keep up. And I don't like being in Tennessee."

Eighteen months ago, when Olivia seemed so excited about this graduate program, I threw myself into supporting her dream. Now it sounds like she is giving up. I'm crushed, not only because Olivia is struggling to the extent that she wants to quit but because I had a dream, too, of seeing her once more on a stage at her graduate school graduation beaming and proud of her accomplishments. And after she finished her graduate degree, she'd have the training needed for an interesting and rewarding career in speech pathology.

Considering the importance of this topic of conversation, I'm surprised that she hangs up quickly after giving me this news. Within a few minutes, I call Olivia back and ask, "Do you need some time off from grad school now? Do you want to go to school in Boston next semester instead? Is it too hard living so far away from home?"

Olivia is quiet and does not respond. I decide not to press her. "Call me back in a few days. Maybe you *do* need to be closer to home and family. Do some research on graduate schools in Boston that offer your degree. Then we can talk more and make a plan."

Olivia murmurs a very quiet, "Okay."

But moments later Olivia calls and, in a barely audible voice, says, "I'm leaving, Mommy."

Over the following days, Olivia doesn't call or answer my calls. I'm beside myself with worry and frustration. Then one day I reach her, but this time instead of being patient and understanding like I intend to be, I'm upset because I feel like I've been cut off and I don't know why. Olivia says that she wants to leave Knoxville in a few days. I'm totally unprepared for this reality. I hang up wondering how this all went so wrong.

Olivia returns to New England, but instead of returning to our home, she goes to live with my parents on the Cape. She does not return my calls. Her silence leaves me shattered. I cannot fall asleep at night and turn to sleeping pills to drown out my anxiety-filled dreams. At work, I go through the motions in a shell-shocked state, desperately trying not to reveal my shattered self to my colleagues. I *really* don't want them to know. I'm living in two worlds—one filled with sadness and anxiety and the other one trying to function competently at work. I don't know how long I can do this.

I'm already dreading Christmas and seeing smiling faces on family-photo Christmas cards and people asking if Olivia will be with me for the holidays. I want to hide. Bury myself under my bedcovers. I feel I've failed as a mother. Why else would Olivia not come home and never call me?

Daily I ask myself, *Why does Olivia seek shelter with my parents? I know that they love her dearly, but why am I summarily excluded?* I don't understand. Has my cherished motherhood ended?

After several weeks, my father calls me on a Sunday afternoon and gives me the first of what become weekly updates about Olivia. This is so strange. I want to hear her voice on the other end of the phone. I want to see her, but Olivia isn't asking.

The long winter months do not bring any reprieve from my suffering. I see myself plummeting like a free diver. But unlike a free diver, who trains for years to prepare her lungs and condition her heart for the life-threatening risks of plunging underwater to extreme depths without a tank, I'm not even remotely prepared. I feel as though I might black out before I fight my way upward to the surface. But I don't want to give up. I fight and fight to push myself up to where I finally surface and desperately fill my burning lungs with air.

After seven months of separation, Olivia asks if I'd like to visit her at my parents' house for Easter. During the two-hour drive to the Cape, I pray that I can connect with Olivia by showing her kindness and love. Olivia also asks me to go to church and listen to her singing in the choir. She has always had a clear, resonant voice. During her solo, tears of joy stream down my face. Olivia and I share a gentle hug following the service. My sister Sarah and her husband, Stephen, join us for the Easter lunch at my parents. Olivia participates in every conversation. I'm relieved that she sounds so much better than she did last fall. The door to improved communications has eased open slightly. After my visit, Olivia and I talk occasionally. For the first time since last fall, I have hope for an improved relationship.

A few months later, in early August, Olivia and I plan to meet again. I drive to Powder Point, the three-mile-long beach in Duxbury that is halfway between where Olivia and I live. I hope to continue to repair our damaged relationship. Olivia gives me a cautious hug; her body contracts as I gently embrace her. We walk from the parking lot to the beach, where we lie down on our towels. In anticipation that it might be difficult to start a conversation, I've brought Olivia one of her favorite magazines, *Coastal Living*, and brought the *Smithsonian* for me. Olivia sees a recipe that she likes and asks if she can keep the magazine.

"Of course. You should try that tasty-looking recipe."

She is very quiet. I try to draw her out by asking about her recent trip with her friend Natalie. "How was your trip to Hawaii? Where did you stay? Were you on a remote island or a large one?"

Olivia answers all my queries in the same measured way, careful not to give me more than I need to know, and careful not to express any emotion. Until, while recollecting a favorite part of her trip, she excitedly tells me that spending the night on a beautiful beach with Natalie's family, sitting around a campfire, and waking to the sounds of the surf was the highlight of her Hawaiian vacation.

We walk along the beach. I watch mothers chasing their toddlers as they rush headlong toward the beckoning waters. Both of my girls used to do this with great glee. I would be giving Olivia a snack on the beach, and then Elizabeth would bolt toward the sea. I'd drop the snack and run after Elizabeth, grab her small hand, and then walk back to Olivia. Moments later with Elizabeth settled on the blanket playing with her bucket and shovel, Olivia would take off toward the waves. I would dash after Olivia, catching her at the water's edge. These were busy and happy times.

"Olivia," I say as I look at her lovingly, "all I really want is for you to be happy. This is what I pray for constantly. This is my *only* wish."

Olivia's shoulders heave as she starts to sob. I rest my hand lightly on her arm. Between her sobs she blurts out, "You used to be so *angry* with me, Mommy. I could never please you. But I hear you now. I do hear you. Thank you, Mommy."

"It's true. I was upset, especially when you left your grad program suddenly and stopped calling me. I was frustrated, hurt, and confused. And even though I tried to find some solutions, like transferring to a similar graduate degree program in the Boston area, it was as though you couldn't take in the offer I made. I felt bruised and defeated."

I glance at my watch. Damn. I'll have to leave soon. I do not want to tell Olivia that three days ago, I had a CT scan of my abdomen to try to diagnose why I've had extreme stomach pain. This morning while I was driving to the beach, I got a call from my primary care doctor, who said I would be hearing from a urologist soon. Moments later, my phone rang again, and an administrator for the urologist asked me to come to his office today.

I'm still confused. Why do I need to speak with a urologist? Shouldn't I be speaking with the doctor who ordered my CT scan? A queasy feeling pulses through me. A doctor's rapid response only means trouble. And now I'm facing a different challenge. Do I tell Olivia that I have an unexpected doctor's appointment? Since Elizabeth's death, she has never liked me to talk about unresolved medical issues, but I decide I have to.

"Olivia, I need to leave in about twenty minutes. I got a call from a doctor's office this morning, and they want to fit me in for a visit at two o'clock."

Olivia starts breathing rapidly, and then she breathes in and out deeply in a measured way. Now, because I have to leave, I've hurt her feelings, which is the last thing I want to do. "I'm sorry, honey. This is something that I need to do."

Olivia walks into the water for a few minutes and when she returns says, "Then let's go."

This is so, so hard.

Surprisingly, when we arrive in the parking lot, Olivia turns to me and says, "This visit went better than I expected, Mommy. I hope your doctor's appointment goes well."

I well up with tears. "I love you, Olivia."

After a moment's pause, Olivia reaches out and hugs me. "I hope you have a happy birthday on Monday, Mommy."

Dr. Closs is a kindly looking man in his early forties. In a soft-spoken voice, he explains to me what the CT scan revealed. "You have a growth in your left kidney. A tumor."

Not what I expected to hear at all. Not what I want to hear. This cannot be right. I ask, "Is this a growth on the outside of my kidney? Couldn't it just be a cyst?"

"No. The growth is inside your left kidney. It has an irregular shape, and based on seeing hundreds of images like yours, there's an eighty percent chance that it is malignant."

I feel blood throbbing in my temples as I learn about the pros and cons of having a biopsy or choosing to have surgery right away. In a cracking voice I say, "You don't know this, but my daughter Elizabeth died from osteosarcoma when she was only fourteen years old. The biopsy sounds as invasive as the surgery. I can't take any risks. I need you to remove this tumor."

I'm trembling and crying. Dr. Closs sincerely expresses his sympathy and then calmly continues to give me more information. But I can't hear him anymore. I'm done. It's too much. I cannot bear any more bad news.

As I walk down the hall to find the administrator who will schedule my pre-op appointment and date of surgery, I say to myself, *Pull yourself together. You can do this. Hold it inside. Hold it inside. Go down the elevator. Pay for the valet parking. Give the man your receipt. Get into your car. Stay calm. Concentrate.*

I climb into my car and enter the pulsing, hectic Friday-afternoon traffic. A car cuts me off. What the hell is *his* hurry? Just get home. Just get home. I know the way. I know the way home. To where I am loved. To where I will be wrapped in Henry's bearlike hug. To where I can sink my fingers into Charlie's soft-as-a-lamb's fur. To my peaceful garden.

Somehow, I've made it home. I lie under our towering maple tree, look up into the beautiful leafy canopy, and breathe in the warm, humid air of this summer's afternoon. Inhale, exhale. Inhale, exhale. Gentle Spirit, comfort me.

That night, I call Olivia and tell her that I have a growth in my kidney and that it will need to be removed. I'm careful not to mention the word *malignant*. She says, "I'm so sorry, Mommy." Then I tell my family and close friends about my news. Everyone responds with offers of help and expressions of love.

Henry and I had planned a vacation months ago to visit friends in Colorado. We decide that it will help us to get away, so the next day, we fly west. We land in Denver and drive two hours north to the home of our friends Carol and Jack in Eagle-Vail. Their Swiss chalet–style house looks onto a verdant golf course and the foothills of the nearby Rocky Mountains. A stream runs between their land and the golf fairway. The sound of water flowing soothes me that night.

The following morning, I look out my window at the azure-blue sky and the fluttering aspen leaves and feel a sense of peace and connection to the beauty of this territory. The spirit of the mountains says to me, *Come and discover my magnificent beauty.*

The following day is my fifty-third birthday. It's filled with calls from my family, each sending me loving wishes for a special day. We drive twenty minutes to Minturn, an old mining and railway town, and set off for a hike. Soon we are hiking up a narrow, two-foot-wide rocky trail into the mountains. Pausing, I see the carcass of a large animal. The vertebrae, ribs, and scapula are all that is left. These mountains are home to many, but I am reminded that we are only guests.

Unaccustomed to this high altitude, Henry and I huff and puff while our hosts stride on. They are strong hikers acclimatized to their surroundings. At the next rise, I pause to look around me and breathe in the beauty of my surroundings. At the edge of the trail, hummingbirds dart in and around the yellow, cone-shaped wild-flowers, a stream runs briskly over rocks, bushes burst with ripe raspberries, and a towering rocky mountain in front of us provides a majestic backdrop. After our hike, Jack drives us up a winding road to a restaurant, where we have lunch outside, overlooking a pan-oramic view of the terracotta foothills of the Rocky Mountains. Later that evening, Henry treats us all to a sumptuous dinner at an Italian restaurant in Vail.

After dinner, I read the birthday cards from Hannah and her family. In large letters my eight-year-old grandson writes, "You are the best. Love, Ben." Six-year-old Chloe's message is "You are so thot-fole." Hannah translates: "You are so thoughtful." Hannah and Will's card says, "Much love from all of us!" I read Chloe's closing message, "You are in your fifdes." Then Olivia calls to wish me a happy birthday. Her voice is upbeat. I sense optimism about a new chapter beginning in her life. Before we hang up, she says, "I love you, Mommy."

Warmly I reply, "I love you too, honey."

I've faced so many storms and many rocks blocking my path, but I've learned to weather the storms and to climb over and around the rocks. I've learned to stop and rest by a flowing stream, to rejoice in the glory of brightly colored wildflowers, and at night, to peer into a thicket of stars on a cloudless night. I am part of this world. Part of the running streams, part of the flickering sunlight on aspen leaves, part of the weather-beaten hillsides, part of the baking midday heat, part of the cool night breezes and midnight-blue sky. No nightmare, no illness can separate me from the loving Spirit who surrounds me, who comforts me, who breathes renewing strength into me.

Chapter 35

September

Fall 2012

I'm sitting outside at home, listening to the cicadas sing their nightly song. A mild, humid breeze falls softly on my face. I'm trying to process the sadness I'm feeling tonight in a healing outdoor place. But it's not working. My soft animal body is torn and tender. It's trying to recover after being penetrated by surgical knives and clamps and sewn up with stitches. My wounds are weeping as much as I am tonight.

I miss Elizabeth. I miss how she wrapped her arms around my neck when we said good night. I miss her gentle voice calling to me from the adjacent room at night. I miss her laughter, her friends, and their silly antics. I miss watching her swim rapidly down the racing lane. I miss when she was eight and she pulled carrots out of our vegetable garden and said, "Carrots taste better with dirt on them." I miss pushing her on a swing and the songs that we used to make up and sing. I miss watching her smile when she ate warm crème brûlée. I miss when she walked her hamster, Hammy, on a leash. I miss being her mom.

And I wonder. How did Elizabeth at only age thirteen cope with her cancer diagnosis and treatments? She had waves of anxiety and anger, but she didn't despair. Her radiant smile lifted the spirits of everyone around her, her humor caught people by surprise, and her empathy gave comfort to other suffering children. Can I be as strong as Elizabeth was? Can I summon my courage to acknowledge my illness and still forge ahead? Can I be as brave as my youngest daughter and live a full life with kindness and joy?

In the weeks that follow, I ponder these questions. After receiving my cancer diagnosis, I was in shock for a few days. I felt queasy and didn't sleep well. I lost my appetite. My anxiety was on high alert. But a shift happened when I was in the Colorado Rockies. I drew great comfort from being in a world created millions of years ago. I imagined being part of a vast eternal world. I no longer felt alone and vulnerable, but part of creation.

Now at home, I practice meditations about belonging to a much larger, more connected world than my own. This practice helps to dissolve my anxiety and empower feelings of connection to a universe where all are welcome and belong: the frail, the strong, the anxious, the bold, the foolhardy, the wise, the insecure, the confident. I understand that we are all integral to the well-being of the whole.

In late September, Olivia visits me on a warm and sunny day. We sit outside, side by side, on chaise lounges like we used to do. She talks about her years in college, how she loved living in a beautiful city by the sea, the subjects she liked to study the most, and the many friends that she made. We remember when I visited her in Charleston and the alluring beach that we frequented. We remember one of our favorite times, when we were whisked along in a tide ride, and when we saw porpoises jumping clear of the water and then gracefully submerging themselves again. We can all but smell the salty air, feel the sand on our toes and the sun on our backs.

Olivia tells me that she will be leaving her grandparents' home soon, and she plans to move in with a friend. She shares ideas that she has for work, and we discuss how she may be able to find a position that will suit her well. It seems as though after a year of struggles and pain, we have found equilibrium again. Before she leaves, she hugs me and says, "I love you, Mommy."

"I love you too, honey."

The following day, I sit on my outdoor chaise lounge and look at my garden. It's one of my favorite pastimes during my recovery. I watch the monarch butterflies in their sheer-spotted frocks of gold, orange, and brown delicately land on the lavender-blue blossoms of the Buddleia and draw in sweet nectar. I catch a glimpse of an emerald-green ruby-throated hummingbird buzzing by with wings rapidly beating. On the highest limbs of the bowing branches of the weeping cherry tree, I see yellow finches with accents of black waiting for their opportunity to gather seed from the nearby feeder.

My mind wanders back in time. I viscerally remember when Elizabeth left this world at this time when the earth begins to rotate away from the sun, when monarch butterflies and ruby-throated hummingbirds gather needed nourishment because they, too, are about to leave me. Only the finches, cardinals, and chickadees will accompany me through the fall and winter.

Now, eleven years later, truth is patiently revealing its secrets. One cannot hold on to despair any more than a butterfly can stop its pulsing wings. One cannot suppress hope any more than a bird can stop its soaring flight. Now I understand that it is up to you and to me to heal, to repair our wounded souls.

So now, in these still moments, let the graceful movements of a delicate butterfly, the awesome swiftness of an emerald-and-ruby hummingbird, and the resplendence of our cherished world fill our shadows with light.

Epilogue

O ver the years, as I walked along woodland paths or by the sea, a latent wish kept emerging. How could I help those who are struggling, who are overwhelmed, who are bearing the unbearable? How could I bring them even a small measure of comfort and hope?

After years of ruminating, an idea started percolating. On my journey, I discovered that writing down what I was not even willing to utter helped to bring about my transformation. I had to bring forth painful memories, dashed dreams, and even nightmares and not keep them buried inside. In this process, I grieved, screamed, questioned, sobbed. In time, I wrote about lessons I learned from Elizabeth and how my community of family and friends rescued me. Slowly, I began to accept that while Elizabeth's illness had taken her life, her brave and compassionate spirit would never die.

What if I could bring this idea of a daily writing practice to parents and their children at a pediatric hospital? What if they discovered that writing could benefit them? I summoned my courage and spoke to a committee of parents and medical professionals at a pediatric hospital. I asked if I could initiate a journal-writing program and encourage parents and their adolescent children to write expressively about their hopes and fears, challenges and victories, courage and compassion. I shared with the committee evidence from research studies that indicated that people who wrote about their experiences while having major health challenges had better physical and psychological outcomes. The committee responded to my idea with a resounding "Yes!"

Once a week I board a train bound for Boston with dozens of journals in tow. On the hospital floors, I meet with family members and adolescent children and speak about the therapeutic benefits of a daily writing practice. To date, the majority of parents and children with whom I speak have expressed an interest in writing.

Now, I am honoring both Elizabeth and my wish. Journals of Hope is thriving.

If you would like to learn more about therapeutic writing programs, please contact me at www.faithwilcoxnarratives.com, www.facebook.com/FaithFWilcox, on Instagram @faith.wilcox, or on Twitter @faithfwilcox.

Notes

Chapter 33

[1] Eden Steinberg, ed. *The Pocket Pema Chödrön*, 2008. Boston: Shambhala Publications, 2008.

Acknowledgments

First of all, I thank my daughter Olivia, whose compassionate, loving care for her little sister was a beacon of light even on the darkest days. In the daily ways she still honors her sister, she demonstrates that the love they shared will never end.

To my husband, Henry, who wholeheartedly encouraged me to write my memoir and whose upbeat, loving energy and endearing ways comfort and support me every day. To my stepchildren and grandchildren, who bring sparkles of happiness into my life.

To my writing coach and editor, Cindy Barrilleaux, who expertly guided me during the book-writing process and who helped me to write coherently even about my shock-blurred memories. Sometimes uncompromisingly direct but always kind, Cindy empowered me to share my story to the best of my ability. And to my second editor, Candace Johnson, who capably reviewed my final manuscript.

I would like to thank the community that supported all of us during Elizabeth's illness and after her death. The medical professionals, including hospice nurses, who expertly and kindly cared for Elizabeth and who counseled Olivia and me. Ministers and therapists who listened to our unanswerable, heartbreaking questions and didn't try to fix us but simply carried some of our unbearable pain.

My college friends, church community, and even some whom I barely knew who contributed funds to pay for uncovered medical costs.

Friends and neighbors of mine and my sisters, who made countless meals for us, gave us rides, and supported us in unending ways. Mothers of Elizabeth's friends who spent many nights in the hospital. Elizabeth's and Olivia's friends who made my daughters laugh with their silly antics, who invited them to their homes to hang out on good days, and who sat by Elizabeth's bedside expressing their love until the last few days before her death.

My friends Beth, Diana, Lisa, Molly, and Nandy, and my cousin Julia, for whom my appreciation will never end. And a special note of thanks to Nandy, who edited an earlier version of my manuscript.

My mother and father, who are known to their grandchildren as Nana and Grampy, for their attentiveness and gifts of rest and restoration during Elizabeth's illness and for their steadfast and loving presence in our lives. My sister Sarah and her husband, Stephen, who formed an especially close bond with Olivia and Elizabeth and lifted our spirits with frequent visits and reasons for hope. My sister Susie and her husband, Peter, who shared their home with Elizabeth, Olivia, and me for eight months while Elizabeth was in treatment and who gave us love and support in innumerable ways. And to Susie, who left her financial services work to care for us during Elizabeth's yearlong illness and who started Hats for Healing, an endeavor in which she made more than two thousand hats and gave the proceeds to help my family. And to my niece Robin and my nephews, Dave and Jon, who were in middle and elementary school when we lived with them, who showed daily acts of kindness, shared their mother and father without complaint, and who brought fun into our lives with their youthful energy.

Finally, I'm grateful to volunteer at the hospital where Elizabeth received world-class care. This opportunity empowers me to give to others who are suffering and, in doing so, honor Elizabeth, who brought happiness, love, and compassion to so many.

About the Author

© Lucian Snow

Faith Fuller Wilcox believes that self-expression through writing leads to healing. Her writing is reflective of a growing body of medical research about "narrative identity," which highlights that how we make sense of what happens to us and the value we give to experiences beyond our control directly impact our physical and psychological outcomes. Faith learned these truths firsthand when her thirteen-year-old daughter, Elizabeth, was diagnosed with a rare bone cancer that took her life. Faith's journey from grief and despair to moments of comfort and peace taught her life-affirming lessons, which she shares today through her writing. Faith is the author of *Facing into the Wind: A Mother's Healing After the Death of Her Child*, a book of poetry designed to be a companion to those who are on the journey of grieving and healing. Faith leads a journal-writing program, Journals of Hope, for pediatric patients and their families, designed to give participants the opportunity to express themselves, alleviate stress, celebrate victories, and honor their grief.

SELECTED TITLES FROM SHE WRITES PRESS

Breathe: A Memoir of Motherhood, Grief, and Family Conflict by Kelly Kittel $16.95, 978-1-93831-478-0
A mother's heartbreaking account of losing two sons in the span of nine months—and learning, despite all the obstacles in her way, to find joy in life again.

Expecting Sunshine: A Journey of Grief, Healing, and Pregnancy after Loss by Alexis Marie Chute $16.95, 978-1-63152-174-4
A mother's inspiring story of surviving pregnancy following the death of one of her children at birth.

Rethinking Possible: A Memoir of Resilience by Rebecca Faye Smith Galli $16.95, 978-1-63152-220-8
After her brother's devastatingly young death tears her world apart, Becky Galli embarks upon a quest to recreate the sense of family she's lost—and learns about healing and the transformational power of love over loss along the way.

The First Signs of April: A Memoir by Mary-Elizabeth Briscoe $16.95, 978-1631522987
Briscoe explores the destructive patterns of unresolved grief and the importance of connection for true healing to occur in this inspirational memoir, which weaves through time to explore grief reactions to two very different losses: suicide and cancer.

Filling Her Shoes: Memoir of an Inherited Family by Betsy Graziani Fasbinder $16.95, 978-1-63152-198-0
A "sweet-bitter" story of how, with tenderness as their guide, a family formed in the wake of loss and learned that joy and grief can be entwined cohabitants in our lives.

Three Minus One: Parents' Stories of Love & Loss edited by Sean Hanish and Brooke Warner $17.95, 978-1-938314-80-3
A collection of stories and artwork by parents who have suffered child loss that offers insight into this unique and devastating experience.